2nd Edition

undecided.

2nd Edition

undecided.

navigating life and learning after high school

Genevieve Morgan

ZEST BOOKS
MINNEAPOLIS

Zest Books™
An imprint of Lerner Publishing Group, Inc.
241 First Avenue North
Minneapolis, MN 55401 USA

For reading levels and more information, look up this title at www.lernerbooks.com.
Visit us at zestbooks.net. 🯀🯀

Cover photo by Annalisa Linn.

Main body text set in Bembo Std.
Typeface provided by Monotype Typography.

Library of Congress Cataloging-in-Publication Data

Names: Morgan, Genevieve, author.
Title: Undecided : navigating life and learning after high school / Genevieve Morgan.
Other titles: Navigating life and learning after high school
Description: 2nd Edition. | Minneapolis : Zest Books, 2020. | Revised edition of the author's Undecided, [2014] | Includes bibliographical references and index. | Audience: Ages 14–18 | Audience: Grades 10–12 | Summary: "This updated and revised edition gives teens a comprehensive overview of the choices available to them after graduating high school, from colleges to workforce, and advice on how to follow each path"— Provided by publisher.
Identifiers: LCCN 2019049785 (print) | LCCN 2019049786 (ebook) | ISBN 9781541597785 (library binding) | ISBN 9781541597792 (paperback) | ISBN 9781728401652 (ebook)
Subjects: LCSH: Student aspirations—Juvenile literature. | Student aspirations —United States—Juvenile literature. | Vocational guidance—United States—Juvenile literature. | College student orientation—United States—Juvenile literature. | Career development—United States—Juvenile literature. | Career education—United States—Juvenile literature. | High school graduates—Life skills guides—Juvenile literature.
Classification: LCC LB1027.8 .M67 2020 (print) | LCC LB1027.8 (ebook) | DDC 331.702/33—dc23

LC record available at https://lccn.loc.gov/2019049785
LC ebook record available at https://lccn.loc.gov/2019049786

Manufactured in the United States of America
1-47922-48368-4/3/2020

Not I, nor anyone else can travel that road for you.
You must travel it by yourself.
It is not far. It is within reach.
Perhaps you have been on it since you were born, and did not know.
Perhaps it is everywhere—on water and land.

—Walt Whitman, *Leaves of Grass*

ACKNOWLEDGMENTS

This book exists thanks to Dan Harmon and Jan Hughes, who were my original editors at Zest Books, and the advisory teen peer group that supported its development along the way. The revised edition came into being under Lerner Publishing Group, who saw the value in my updating the original. My sincere thanks to editors Hallie Warshaw, Ashley Kuehl, and Andrea Nelson at Lerner/Zest for recognizing the importance in evolving this book and working diligently with me to help it meet the needs of a changing world.

A big thanks to Kate Coon, Holly Bull, Aidan Rooney, Doug Drew, Penelope Trunk, and John C. McCain for contributing their insights culled from years and years of guiding young people through this bewildering transition. To Andrew Thompson for his help with some of the research. Gratitude to all of you teachers, students, and parents who shared your personal stories of indecision with me. May you embrace the future with gusto!

And finally, thanks to my sons, Graham and Wyeth, who followed the advice in this book and threw themselves into uncertainty after high school to discover themselves. It's been a joy to watch you become the young men I always hoped you'd be. Thank you for proving my point.

contents

Introduction

So here you are, approaching the end of high school. Endings are hard, even if you didn't like high school all that much. Endings signal a transition and a need to let go of old ideas and start something new. The problem comes when you have no clue about what that something new is—and that is most of us right now. I'm writing this in the midst of the COVID-19 pandemic and the largest unemployment numbers since the Great Depression, so there is hardly a soul around who is decided about much when it comes to the near future. There's nothing like social isolation and the collapse of the economy to show us how fragile herd mentality is. Instead of looking to others to define our goals (following the herd), we have a unique opportunity right now to look inside and define our goals on our own terms. And that is what this book is here to help you do. Inner exploration can be a source of a lot of anxiety, or, if you hang in there with me, a fertile field of possibility and indomitable strength. As we all reckon with the fragility of our institutions (including higher academia), we can wither in fear or we can blossom. My intention is for you to do the latter. Your future success does not rely on outside institutions and peers but on you. Your spirit. Your resilience. Your courage. Your character. In peril and prosperity, if you choose a path that cultivates and empowers your inner qualities, you will thrive. It may not be the path you thought you'd be taking, but that's okay. That's why you are reading this book.

For many of you, college is still the first step on the next path. Maybe you've had to delay touring and applying, but it is still your go-to option for life after high school. And it should be explored fully. The tidal wave of college talk usually starts to build in sophomore year—maybe even freshman year for some. By junior year, it's all many of the adults around you can talk about: schoolwork, ambition, test scores, hobbies, college visits, applications. If you are very lucky, you may already have a good idea about what you want to do when you grow up. Maybe you've always wanted to be a doctor or an actress or a banker or a soldier, and you've been tailoring your high school experience to meet those expectations. But if—like most teens—you are deeply confused or torn, or have absolutely no clue about what you want to do next, then congratulations! You are in exactly the right place. I have written this book for you!

That distinction between what you *want* to do versus what you are *expected* to do is an important one—especially in the United States, where many teens default to college directly after graduating high school.

There are good reasons for this, which I'll talk about in a minute, but when it comes to *you*—your dreams, desires, and passions, your budget, your innate talents, and the things you have worked to get good at—college may or may not be the obvious and natural choice right after graduation. You might be happier taking a year or two to find yourself through work, service, or travel before (or maybe instead of) going to college. In Europe, taking time off to travel and explore is such a common tradition that there is even a name for it: *Wanderjahr*, German for "wandering year." Our concept of a gap year comes from that tradition. You don't have to travel very far anymore to go exploring. You can do almost anything, from learning computer animation to speaking French or perfecting your meditation, via the internet. So don't feel bad if you're undecided. Feel normal.

Amid all this talk of college, I'm sure you're also painfully aware of the huge, green elephant in the middle of the conversation. You know, the one that looks and smells like money—or, more specifically, money you are likely to owe after you graduate. College is just flat-out, incredibly expensive; yet, at the same time, going to college substantially increases career opportunities and earning potential for graduates. So there's the rub. To eventually get a good job (one that will pay off your debts), you have to face going into debt first. And you aren't alone if you are questioning whether the payoff is worth the pinch, even more so now than when *Undecided* was first published in 2015. The intervening years have not been kinder to students—or their debt load—and the news everywhere often reads grim and fatalistic. But on the fabulous and incredible flip side for me (and you, I hope), more students are recognizing the value of acting from a place of integrity, not just reflex. They are embracing the idea of time off after high school to figure out what they really want to do and, therefore, how to get the best value for their investment. And after experiencing a semester or two of remote learning, you are right to ask what, *exactly*, is your tuition paying for? The pandemic has torn the façade off the already questionable practice of plunging our country's future into massive debt.

What I see manifesting all over the place in a way that gives me so much hope is the concept that spawned the original *Undecided*: breaking free of societal and parental expectations and forging a unique path for *yourself*, and in doing so, changing the world for the better. We are on shifting ground as a society, and that means the flexible and adaptable among us will fare the best. Guess what helps you become adaptable and flexible? Being brave enough to question tradition and rigid ideas and forge your own answers. Walk your own path. And face the unpredictable with confidence in your abilities. This book will guide you in all of these things as you become an adult.

When I say "adult," I mean something very specific, not just a chronological age when you can vote or drink or start paying your own bills. That's part of it, sure. But what I *really* mean is the point at which you are able to simply live life on your own terms. Set your own standards. Buy your own food. Pay your own rent. Make your own way by your own lights. This sounds easy enough, but it isn't, especially when you're sitting where you are right now— bewildered, burnt out, and maybe even hostile—with a lot of people filling your ears with their opinions about what you ought to do. In this book, I do my best to make sure you have everything you need to craft your own future—one that reflects *your* values and ambition and feels true to you. Does that mean you won't make mistakes? Of course not. But my hope is that whatever mistakes you make will feel real and ownable, and not foisted on you by other people's drama and unrealistic expectations. And therein, I swear, lies the secret to adult happiness. Part of what makes the next several years feel so important is that they have a deserved reputation as the time when people have the chance to turn the base metal of their intrinsic personalities and ambitions into real-world gold. A career. A skill. An outlook. A *life*. What is just a passing interest in music today could become a career in sound engineering tomorrow. And that math class you hate? It could get you into an economics class that helps you start your own business. You don't know the endgame right now because you are still in the middle of the play. The important thing is to be willing to *get out there*.

You *are* important. Yes, these times are tough, but so are you. You are warriors for the environment, diversity, and equality, and you are legion. So let's face the future together, here, as you approach the end of high school. Let's figure out who you are and what you want to do after high school.

YOU ARE ON A HUMAN PATH

This book comes at a critical juncture in your life, and I hope that it will help you break out of conformity (and perhaps some degree of fear) and into a new idea about yourself, how you can learn, and what you can be in the grown-up world. The K–12 public education system in our country tends to silo kids into different futures based on their standardized test performances and class "tracks." Colleges, too, are hell-bent on making sure you maximize your time there, declare and stick to a major, and graduate with "job-ready skills" to justify their egregious cost hikes. (The average cost of tuition at a public university has risen by 213 percent in the last thirty years. Tuition at a private university has gone up 129 percent.)

But you are not a robot on a track, or a bank account. You are an individual living in a free society and, by the age of eighteen (or before if you are legally emancipated), are considered by that same society to be an independent individual who can make educational and life path decisions for yourself. Your parents, guardians, and teachers may help you in myriad ways, but they can no longer legally control you.

I recommend that you challenge your own idea of who you are and open up to the possibilities the world has to offer. I want you to look forward to your future with a sense of optimism and adventure, not resignation and dread. Your future will be what you make of it. As you mentally go through different scenarios, keep in mind one important thing (and, honestly, most parents would probably agree that this mattered the most at this age): whatever direction you take, make a commitment to yourself to keep challenging yourself after high school. Choose a path that fires up your brain, increases your skills, and helps you gain real experience. Almost every occupation that has a high degree of personal satisfaction (and competitive pay) will require some level of continuing education and hands-on training. *Where* you get that education, *when* you get it, and *how long* it takes you—well, that's a different story. That's what this book will help you sort out.

HOW TO USE THIS BOOK

This book is divided into five sections. The first section is all about you and where you are right now. It is important to read this section first before you go on to the next four sections, which will cover where you may be headed later. This first section is meant to help you in the decision-making process by giving you insight into aspects of your personality, character, and interests. We will also delve into the intimidating financial and family factors that make the process more difficult and try to demystify them to help you plan accordingly.

The next four sections are divided into the possible directions you might take: higher education (read: more school), service (military, civil, volunteer, and community), work (internships, day jobs, and starting your own business), and a hybrid of the above that includes possibilities for gap years or time off. Within each section are some charts and worksheets—though I've tried to keep these down; it's not school after all—where you can record your personal information to refer back to. Additionally, throughout the book you will find helpful sidebars and tips. Don't skip these! They will give you websites or other important information that can streamline your process. And I've also included mini biographies of people who have successfully navigated their way into adulthood, despite a long and twisted path.

I have provided as broad an overview as I can into the whats, wheres, hows, and whys of each option available to you, but be forewarned that there are so many different individual institutions, programs, organizations, incentives, and variations available (and more surfacing every day) that no one book can cover them all without being a snooze-worthy encyclopedia. Enter the internet. Every single selection I cover in this book can be explored in depth by going online and requesting more information, and I encourage you to do so, as much will be changing in the wake of the pandemic. Contact real people in real time through their websites, and they will answer specific questions, especially about travel and safety.

My goal for you, by the time you finish reading this book, is that you be well on your way toward crafting a plan for your life after graduation—a plan that feels exciting and right for you. If you have read this far, I think you're already on the fast track toward that goal. You've identified yourself to be a person who is curious and adventurous about the future. You already know yourself a bit—at least enough to know you are undecided—and that is a perfect place to begin.

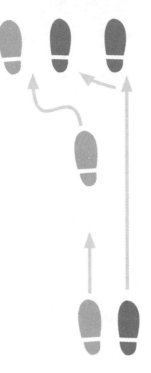

It takes courage to grow up and
become who you really are.

—*ee cummings*

part one:

you are here

What Makes You Tick?

Take a look at your friends and family: They're all really different, right? And not just in a physical sense but also in terms of *who* they are and what they are good at. Maybe one has great taste in clothes, another is the go-to person for notes you missed in history class, or another is a genius at *Call of Duty*. Yet no matter how different we may seem to be, we can also be assured of sharing certain similarities. The way that humans prioritize work and the enthusiasm with which we undertake different tasks has been the subject of much research over the years—and a lot of speculation as well. But it's important when contemplating next moves to think seriously about what kind of a person you are from the inside out (in other words, not who you think you should be or how others perceive you). By understanding the similarities that we have with other humans, we can benefit from their experiences and avoid common pitfalls. Scientists and sociologists call these similarities "personality traits"—and once you know yours, they can serve as signposts to point you in the right direction and make your progress through life just that much smoother.

But don't be fooled: Personality is a hard thing to pin down. It is very complex and always evolving. A host of external factors help to shape it, such as your inherited temperament, your family and social environments, your peers, your education, and your activities; but despite our personal styles and quirks, there are common themes that researchers have been able to identify and measure. Most have to do with how our human brains process and integrate information, which influences emotions and behavior, which then impacts how we interact socially with others. If you were a computer, then your physical body would be your mainframe and your personality traits, or the fundamental psychological factors that shape how you relate to the world, would be similar to your operating system.

Happily, you are a human and not a machine—you have vast and unprogrammable depths—but you can start now to identify certain basic tendencies, or traits, in your personality that will help you understand what you really want out of your life and to make an informed decision about your future. After all, when it really comes down to it, the only difference between doing something you love and doing something you hate is your ability to know what you love and pursue it. Maybe you think you know yourself pretty well by now, but chances are you aren't aware of things going on in your subconscious (the hidden part beneath your conscious mind), as well as habits you've acquired over the years.

TEMPERAMENT

Temperament is the bedrock of personality. It can be hard to differentiate the two, but personality is actually the expression of temperament.

Temperament is defined as the innate emotional activity that we inherit from our parents and is identifiable when we are tiny babies in the way we, say, react to strangers or a change in temperature or light. Temperament can be developed or squashed by the way we are raised, including how receptive our caregivers were to our needs, but it remains our default condition. Some of the characteristics studied in babies that are associated with temperament are:

- Activity levels (relaxed or amped)
- Consistency of habits (sleeping, eating)
- Distractibility
- Sensitivity
- Irritability/frustration
- Persistence
- Approach/withdrawal to novelty

These qualities are, in the very broadest of terms, inherited from your folks and are the psychological hand you are dealt when you come into this world. The more accepting you are of your natural temperament, the easier it will be to create a life that works for you. In other words, you can grow into your personality, but you can't grow out of your temperament.

PERSONALITY TRAITS

Now we wade into deeper waters. Personality traits, which are an expression of temperament, are considered to be intrinsic to who we are and have been studied as a way to categorize people into certain psychological "types." Researchers are consistently coming up with new studies on this topic, but the theory of different kinds of personality types is largely based on psychological preferences that were the brainchild of a Swiss psychiatrist named Carl G. Jung (1865–1961). He worked with Sigmund Freud, who has fallen out of favor these days but is still widely considered to be the father of modern psychiatry.

Jung was a complicated man with a lot of issues. (When he was a child, he used to faint every time he had to go to school or study.) He viewed the human experience as a kind of mythic journey and used the word *archetypes* to describe primordial patterns of behavior that give our lives significance. Behaviorists and psychologists either love him or laugh at him; yet his work lives on and can be a useful lens to look through to see ourselves, our struggles, and how we think. Jung believed that human behavior, varying as it does from individual to individual, is actually the result of major differences in how we use our mental capacities. In his theory, personality is dependent on a temperamental tendency toward external or internal processing, plus other opposing mental functions: the way we *receive* information (sensing or intuition) and the way we *process* information (thinking or feeling). During World War II, two American women, Isabel Briggs Myers and her mother, Katharine Cook Briggs, added a function to Jung's basic theory on personality. They described two ways in which a person might prefer to *classify* information (perceiving or judging).

One personality trait descended from Jung that is very useful to know about yourself is your level of *extroversion* (or its sister, *introversion*). Many psychologists and sociologists consider an individual's natural preference for one over the other as an intrinsic part of their personality. Simply put, these qualities describe how and under what circumstances you tend to get your energy and where you like to put your focus. Everyone comes equipped with both, but individuals tend to express one over the other. Knowing which way you trend is a good baseline.

An **extrovert** is a person who is energized by being around other people; they prefer doing to thinking and like to work out problems by talking about them with other people. Being alone makes them feel apathetic and crabby; they prefer a wide circle of friends, a variety of activities, and a full social calendar.

An **introvert** is a person who gets energized by the life of the mind; they like thinking and exploring their thoughts and feelings. They get drained when they spend too much time in groups of people and often prefer a few deep friendships to the social whirl, with plenty of breaks to just hang out and chill.

You are probably thinking that you and every teenager you know is an extrovert, but remember, extroversion and introversion are traits you've had since birth.

If you were the kind of baby that got overstimulated easily and cried when too many relatives passed you around at Grandma's, you may be a natural introvert who has learned to be extroverted because you simply like people. An introvert is not necessarily somebody who is shy or quiet or a wallflower at parties but somebody who feels *recharged* after spending time alone. In contrast, an extrovert is not necessarily a chatterbox class president or the life of every party but rather is somebody who feels more *alive* after interacting with others. They clear their heads by talking with friends or doing something that engages them externally—like a sport. In other words, an introvert can be social and an extrovert can like to be alone, but that's not where they get their juice. After a few months in social isolation, I bet you have an instinct about whether you tend toward introvert or extrovert, but just in case you don't, take the quiz on pages 24–25 to find out. If you want to dig deeper into the other kinds of personality preferences, check out the websites I've listed in the sidebar on page 26.

Quiz

I

Your best friend just texted to invite you to the beach with some other people. Problem is, you don't have a ride. You:

A. Text back right away: YES! (Rides, schmides. You'll figure it out later.)

B. Wait until you nail down a ride to answer. You don't want to be stuck out there.

2

Your idea of the perfect date is:

A. Dinner at your favorite restaurant, then off to an amusement park or a sporting event where you can meet up with friends and cheer for your favorite team together.

B. A walk on the beach followed by a movie, then dessert at a café where you can dissect the movie together.

3

When you get together with a friend you like to:

A. Go for a run, message friends to see what they're doing (maybe you can hook up with them?), shop, surf the web, and make comments. Talk about anything and everything.

B. Just hang out together, wherever, make something cool, read magazines. You don't always need to talk; it's good just to be together.

4

If you have an empty afternoon, it makes you feel:

A. Stir-crazy. What is everyone else doing?

B. Relieved. Now you can relax.

5

Small-talk for you is:

A. As easy as breathing.

B. Stupid. Why talk when you have nothing interesting to say?

6   Your preferred method of communication is:

   A. Video call. And the person better answer right away!

   B. Message. You can wait for an answer.

7   Your parents just grounded you and you're angry. You:

   A. Tweet about it. Everyone should know how mean they are.

   B. Grab your earbuds and retreat to your room. Who knows when they'll get the pleasure of your company again?

8   You prefer to study:

   A. In study hall.

   B. At home.

9   At the dinner table at home, it's more the case that:

   A. It's hard to get a word in edgewise, but you are always trying.

   B. You learn a lot from the conversation around you.

IO   People tell you that you are a good listener.

   A. Not often, if ever.

   B. All the time.

As _____ **Bs** _____

If you answered mostly As, chances are good you are looking for a party most of the time and have a lot of extrovert qualities. If you answered mostly Bs, you are most likely more introverted and would appreciate a little break from the craziness of the high school social scene. Now that you know, write it down here:

I am more of an _____.

All this talk about personality traits and brain systems only scrapes the surface of the digging you can do into your own tendencies. If you are into this stuff and would really like to know more, there are tons of free tests and explanations online, including a popular one called the Myers-Briggs Type Indicator, available at 16personalities.com, personalitypathways.com, or humanmetrics.com. It is used by a lot of employers, coaches, college admission counselors, and even matchmakers to help understand personality or psychological type and create good fits at work, on teams, in partnerships, and in school. It has its share of detractors, including some serious scientists, so take the results with a grain of salt, and remember what I said about adaptability. If what you read seems apt to you and helpful, then great, but if it doesn't seem to fit, don't worry about it. These sites offer interesting reading regardless of the quizzes, as well as in-depth explanations about the different personality types, why they matter, and how you can best apply the information. They can also help explain why certain traits in your friends or siblings drive you nuts! (It's pretty fun.) You can also go to idrlabs.com/personality-types.php and check out famous people that match your MBTI personality type, which is a crack-up. Like I said, take what's useful and leave the rest.

CORE VALUES

There's a form of cognitive dissonance people encounter at the bitter end of high school. All those people in your life who told you what to do and how to do it when you were younger are now asking you to be self-directed. They use terms like "find your passion" and "get it together," but what they really mean is that it is *your* turn to take the wheel and drive the car that is your destiny. After a lifetime of sleeping in the backseat, you might find yourself feeling frustrated and really anxious by the expectation that you should now, instinctively, know what you want or where you are supposed to go. In the words of an eighteen-year-old I recently spoke to, "I mean, I only know what I know. You know?"

Since the first edition of *Undecided*, I've worked with many students who feel stressed and unhappy because they just don't know what they want, and they don't want to disappoint their parents. I've talked to even more parents who are desperately afraid that one misstep on the path to adulthood might doom their child to a miserable life. The pressure is palpable. When so much is unknown, it triggers a fear response that can become chronic. Anxiety can make itself known in many unpleasant forms including persistent feelings of dread, nervousness and the jitters, frequent panic attacks, headaches, stomach problems, shortness of breath, and fatigue. And it can be absolutely debilitating.

Young people are currently facing a plague of anxiety (and depression and other mental health challenges). In a 2019 Pew survey, 70 percent of teens said anxiety is a major problem among their friends and 26 percent say it's a minor problem. It gets worse among college kids, where 75 percent report overwhelming anxiety, as reported by the 2019 National College Health Assessment. Much of this anxiety is related to grades, pressure to perform academically and athletically, and on social media, which acts like a cancer eating away at self-esteem. There is also the kind of meta-anxiety we are all facing these days that revolves around outsized fears of global pandemic, mass shootings, climate catastrophe, and a sense of world events spinning out of control.

Social media creates the mirage that everyone around you is living a life of effortless perfection—which is a load of crap.

Is it any wonder then that so many teens turn to partying to escape or to self-medicate, or, as my son calls it, Type I fun? The problem here is that smoking pot, doing harder drugs, and drinking might make you feel better for a couple hours, but they actually keep you stuck in the same quagmire of anxiety and depression in the long term—and sometimes pull you deeper. As someone very wise once told me, "It's like every morning you get to walk out the front door into a new day, and walk down the front path toward the road. Then you drink or smoke or whatever, and you wake up the next day and find yourself back on your front stoop. You never make it down the path. You always end up in the same place."

So what *does* work? Learning real tools to cope when anxiety strikes, such as deep breathing techniques, meditation, and reorienting, that can actually counteract the fear response—or kicking it up a notch and finding a mental health professional or counseling group to help you work through some of these behaviors and feelings. On a macro level, aligning your behavior with your *core values*—or what really matters to you right now—is an anxiety-squelcher. It will cut through a lot of mind tricks and BS from other people and help you make tracks down that front path. You may never be able to control outside events, but if you start honing in on who *you* are and what is important to you, you'll know you can trust yourself to act with clarity and integrity and not cheat yourself of your momentum. This is real strength, and strength is the antidote to fear.

looking back

"Identifying my core values totally helped me at a really hard time in my life. I was feeling conflicted and confused and burnt out with academics and wanted a change. But my parents were really anxious and nervous about me getting off the track they had envisioned for me. So figuring out where I was truly coming from at that moment helped me talk to myself about who I was and to communicate with my parents about my priorities and what I was thinking about doing. This helped ratchet down the tension between us so I felt more supported and they felt less worried all the time."

—*N. Craig, recent college graduate*

IDENTIFYING YOUR CORE VALUES

Core values are the fundamental beliefs of a person or an organization. If you ever work for a big corporation, you will hear this term discussed often between team leaders as they strive to create authentic identities for their brand. In school you might have done some similar exercises to build your emotional literacy. I know you are probably thinking to yourself right now, *This is dumb; I know what I'm about*, but bear with me and ask yourself, do you? I mean, really? Enough to tell me what your core values are and how your actions represent those beliefs? If so, I give you permission to skip this section . . . but if you can't quote me your personal mission statement in an elevator the next time I meet you, read on. (Mine is "Be kind and follow through," in case you were asking.)

Right now, right this minute, get your phone and stop following anyone on social media who regularly guts your self-esteem, at least until you finish this book. Block them, mute them, whatever you need to do, but get off the torture train. In fact, stop paying so much attention to society's external mirrors, and start paying a lot more attention to your internal reflection. You are the only one who can do this next part, and it's hard, but if you start trying to figure out who you really are and what you really like now, you will save a huge amount of time, and your anxiety will improve. The challenge is to integrate that ideal and live it—and by no means does the process look like anything on Instagram. One study published in the *Journal of Social and Clinical Psychology*—"Seeing Everyone Else's Highlight Reels: How Facebook Usage Is Linked to Depressive Symptoms"—looked at how college students' social comparison via social media impacted their psychological health and concluded that "people feel depressed after spending a great deal of time on Instagram or Snapchat because they feel bad when comparing themselves to others." Not a lightbulb moment for most of us, but it is useful to know that a step out of the darkness is to put down your phone. Stop watching what other people are posting, and go out and do some of your own stuff. And to pay it forward, be mindful of how often you are crafting your own posts to make it look like you are living large. Above all, please remember this quote by the wonderful writer and coach Byron Katie: "Reality is always kinder." Our minds tend to go to the worst places, but reality never feels as bad as we think it will.

Once you ground yourself in what is important to you, it is way easier to tune out the rest of the clutter coming at you and make some choices that will be truly productive and happy-making.

WHAT ARE YOUR CORE VALUES?

Here is a long list of words that represent certain behaviors and beliefs you might have about yourself. I'd like you take a pen or pencil and write down ten of them that really resonate with you—the person you feel you are or want to be.

- Academic
- Active
- Affluent
- Aggressive
- Athletic
- Authentic
- Authoritative
- Balanced
- Bold
- Brainy
- Brave
- Calm
- Careful
- Chaste
- Cheerful
- Clever
- Committed
- Communal
- Compassionate
- Competent
- Confident
- Consistent
- Creative
- Credible
- Curious
- Daring
- Dependable

- Determined
- Diligent
- Dutiful
- Efficient
- Ethical
- Extroverted
- Fair
- Faithful
- Family-oriented
- Fit
- Fluid
- Friendly
- Fun-loving
- Funny
- Gentle
- Giving
- Grateful
- Harmonious
- Honest
- Honorable
- Independent
- Influential
- Innovative
- Insightful
- Intelligent
- Intrepid
- Introverted

- Intuitive
- Just
- Kind
- Loving
- Loyal
- Motivated
- Nurturing
- Obedient
- Original
- Open
- Outdoorsy
- Passionate
- Peaceful
- Persistent
- Playful
- Popular
- Positive
- Powerful
- Progressive
- Purposeful
- Reliable
- Religious
- Respectful
- Responsible
- Secure
- Self-reliant
- Simple
- Solitary
- Spiritual
- Spontaneous
- Stable
- Successful
- Tidy
- Traditional
- Trustworthy
- Wealthy
- Wise

Out of these ten words, circle five that feel the most true or valuable to you right now. You can keep the other five in the back of your mind, especially if they represent qualities you aspire to. The five you are left with are your five most important core values at this point in your life, and any decision you make over the next couple of years should be rooted in these qualities, or at least pay real respect to them. For example, if *passionate*, *bold*, *original*, *fun-loving*, and *spontaneous* are your core values, any college you might apply to should reflect these values, and any alternative plan you are thinking about should be flexible, challenging, and inspiring, without a lot of scheduled obligations.

profile

Ellen DeGeneres, comedian, actor, writer, TV show host

Ellen DeGeneres was never thought of as "the funny one" in her family. That accolade went to her older brother, Vance. When DeGeneres was a teenager, she wanted to be a veterinarian, but she didn't think she was smart enough. Instead, she spent one semester as a communications major at the University of New Orleans before dropping out. She went through a lot of entry-level jobs: she waited tables, shucked oysters, worked retail, sold vacuum cleaners, painted houses, and worked as a legal secretary (bumming out about the rigid business dress code) before she came to the conclusion that other people's rules were not a good fit and she would have to make a career for herself that was self-directed. Her big breakthrough came after she was asked to speak at a public engagement. She was so nervous that she started cracking jokes just to get through the speech. People actually laughed—a lot—and she received a few invitations to do local stand-up comedy.

She began performing professionally in 1981, at the age of 23, with the financial and moral support of her mom. Five years later, a talent scout from *The Tonight Show Starring Johnny Carson* came to see one of her shows and invited her to appear on TV. She nailed it and became the first female comedian to be invited to sit on Carson's famous couch. She starred in the eponymous hit sitcom, *Ellen*, until 1998. In 1997 she came out as gay on her TV show and became a vocal advocate of LGBTQ rights. This may not seem all that noteworthy now, but it was a controversial move back in those days, and she suffered serious backlash. Her show was canceled over it—even though she won an Emmy that year. In 2003 DeGeneres made a huge comeback and began hosting her own talk show, the massively popular *The Ellen Degeneres Show*, which is still on the air today. In 2016 President Obama gave DeGeneres the Presidential Medal of Freedom in recognition of her talent and her long-standing support of LGBTQ rights. She has said, "I think by being truthful, and being honest, that saved me."

WHY SHOULD YOU CARE?

No person is a static being locked into their behavior. Your preferences will evolve throughout your entire life. What's useful at this moment is to see if there's a pattern or tendency that can serve as a guide along the way. Take, for example, a leadership seminar I once attended where the organizer split the room up into two groups of people: those who rolled their toothpaste tube up neatly from the bottom and those who smushed it haphazardly in the middle. Turns out, I'm a smusher, big time, and smushers tend to drive rollers crazy. At the very least, I learned never to marry a roller. I also learned that I would not be happy in my work if the role I had was inflexible, exacting, or strictly monitored. In other words, I would make a lousy air traffic controller. Does this mean I will never choose to roll up the toothpaste tube from the bottom? No. But it means that it's not my preference, it does not come naturally, and I am a way happier person if it's not an issue with the people I work and live with. So use this information going forward as a basic guide. If you are more of an introvert who likes a consistent schedule and one of your core values is creativity, making a loose plan that never leaves you any time for solitude or imagination will make you miserable; and if you are an extrovert motivated by being popular and entertaining, too much alone time will make you feel lonely.

What Do You Love to Do?

Now we are going to move from theories about the individual (you) to theories about the group (everyone else you come in contact with). If the information in the previous chapter revealed a little more about your *personal* identity, the material in this chapter should reveal more about your *social* identity. Experts in group dynamics call this *social orientation*.

In plain English, this translates to: how much of your own individual ground are you willing to sacrifice for the betterment of others in your group? Nicholas Lore, a very successful career coach and founder of an organization called the Rockport Institute, breaks it down into two general descriptions, sort of like PCs and Macs.

Communal People These people get the biggest buzz out of being a part of an organization or group. They absorb many of their values, goals, and perspectives from the group they're in. Most of us are communal (three out of four), probably because the survival of our species relied on a majority of our prehistoric ancestors sticking together. (It would have been a lot easier for a saber-tooth tiger to pick off a lone wanderer than to attack the group.)

Maestros These are the exceptions and make up the other 25 percent of the population: the bold outliers. These people march to their own beat and don't require fitting into the group to feel happy or whole. They often have very specialized interests, expertise, or knowledge, and by high school their unique talents are pretty clear to everyone around them. While they don't need to be popular, they do like to be acknowledged for the special contributions they make.

It's pretty easy to know whether you are more of a communal person or a maestro by your own social tendencies. Observe how you feel *more* often. Nobody is just one thing, so a communal person can have maestro leanings and vice versa. The thing to look for is what you prefer more or most of the time. If you suffer from FOMO (fear of missing out), if it feels more comfortable for you to go with the flow of your group, or if you can say you *have* a group, it's likely you are more communal. If you are more of a lone wolf and like to do your own thing, regardless of where the crowd wants to go, you are more likely a maestro.

IT'S YOUR PARTY

In his book, *Now What? The Young Person's Guide to Choosing the Perfect Career,* Lore came up with the following four basic personality types that combine an essential aspect of your personality (introversion or extroversion) and an essential preference in groups (communal or maestro). This is very basic information about yourself that will give you a hint as to your preferred social scene and how you recharge—but it is top level. To refine it, you will have to do more specific research about yourself on your own.

Choose the definition you think is the *most* like you right now:

Introverted Communal	Extroverted Communal
Introverted Maestro	Extroverted Maestro

As I've pointed out, there are a lot of other traits to take into account. For our purposes, however, it's enough information to begin the decision-making process. I stress the word *begin*. The next several years are about exploration and experimentation; the last thing I want to do is have you label yourself in some kind of lasting way.

Our ultimate goal is to understand the underlying forces that influence what you do and why, and what kinds of experiences are in your comfort zone. Once we have that solid footing, you are going to use the rest of the book to imagine scenarios that will challenge that comfort zone. It's a balancing act, and part of becoming an adult is learning when to take risks and when to retreat into safety and ask for help. I'm trying to save you a lot of time and

profile

Paul Orfalea, founder of Kinko's

If you told a teenage Paul Orfalea that soon he would found the most successful copy-store chain in the country, he probably would have laughed. By the end of high school, things did not look great on the academic front. Orfalea was labeled severely learning disabled: a D-minus student who suffered from undiagnosed and untreated ADHD and dyslexia. In the classroom, he was a mess by school standards: He couldn't read or sit still. His mind and his tongue raced. He was restless and hyper and flunked two grades before getting expelled from several schools. He's been quoted saying, "I'm not good at being at work—I'm good at getting out of work." His best class in school was wood shop.

It was this restlessness that helped Orfalea build a fledgling copy store—a store he started in 1970 with a $5,000 bank loan cosigned by both his parents—into a business that sold to FedEx for $2.4 billion in 2004. That road began when, after barely graduating high school, he realized he had only two choices: go into the military or go to college. He chose college and started taking classes at a local community college. Then, after consulting an admissions officer at the University of Southern California, he was allowed to transfer there on the condition that he would only attend USC Extension, or night school. Orfalea couldn't believe the long lines of students waiting for the Xerox machine in the USC library—or that they were willing to pay ten cents per photocopy. He got the loan and set up his first store, selling stationery and offering copy machine services at less than three cents per page. Within ten years, his company had expanded to eighty stores. He couldn't bear staying inside the office, so he made it his business to go store to store and see what was happening. He turned his weaknesses into strengths and didn't let poor grades get in the way. As he says, "There's more to life than what goes down on a report card."

grief in this chapter by helping you understand what makes you feel safe and why. That way, you can have the confidence to break out and try new things even if they feel a little risky or uncomfortable at first.

YOUR INTERESTS

Next, let's find out more about what you like to do with your time off—not what adults think you should do but what you actually prefer to do when you have some empty hours and are left alone to decide how to fill them. Now, I know that if you only had a few days, you might like to sleep until noon, hang out with your friends, and eat takeout every night, but I'm not talking about that. That's vacation. I'm talking about what you would do *after* you got sick and tired of chilling out. If you discovered other interests while you were stuck at home during the COVID-19 pandemic (for instance, baking bread or sewing or building bookshelves), keep them in mind for this next part.

Listed on the following pages are activities that teens do when they have time to themselves. Pick at least five that you are most likely to do.

Check Yourself!

- ☐ Read
- ☐ Work out
- ☐ Post on social media
- ☐ Browse the internet
- ☐ Watch videos or movies
- ☐ Draw or paint
- ☐ Play sports
- ☐ Play video games
- ☐ Call or message friends
- ☐ Fix something in your room or around the house
- ☐ Write a letter or email to someone you haven't seen in a long time
- ☐ Redecorate your room
- ☐ Organize your shelves and/ or closet

- ☐ Make lists of things to do for school or after-school activities
- ☐ Run or walk in nature
- ☐ Clean or do other chores
- ☐ Play with a pet
- ☐ Play with a younger sibling
- ☐ Make up new outfits to wear
- ☐ Go biking or skateboarding
- ☐ Write
- ☐ Create beats/write songs
- ☐ Help a friend or set people up on a date
- ☐ Take apart or fix something mechanical
- ☐ Build something
- ☐ Attend a protest or grassroots organization meeting

- [ ] Make playlists for yourself or to share with friends

- [ ] Plant something

- [ ] Knit, felt, or crochet

- [ ] Get a jump on your homework

- [ ] Trick out your gear (bike, skateboard, snowboard, etc.)

- [ ] Create a show or dance routine

- [ ] Daydream or plan for the future

- [ ] Cook or bake

- [ ] Practice a musical instrument

- [ ] Practice a foreign language

- [ ] Make up a science experiment

- [ ] Take and edit photographs

- [ ] Make jewelry or other crafts

- [ ] Take practice SAT or ACT tests

- [ ] Go to a yoga class

- [ ] Make up a crossword puzzle or other game

- [ ] Write computer code

- [ ] Volunteer to help out a neighbor or organization

- [ ] Solve a difficult equation or puzzle

- [ ] Fix up an old car or motorbike

- [ ] Put together LEGO models or other assemblage kits

Now take a look at what you've checked—and make a mental note about whether they actually correspond to the core values you just identified. Is there any common ground? Are you doing them because you want to or because you think they look good to others and will make your parents proud? Sit with this for a minute, because when we talk about making a plan for after high school, it should be one that comes from you and is for you—not somebody else's idea for you.

Generally speaking, teens fall into several categories when it comes to interests. These categories overlap a lot and are mutually interdependent, so don't go pigeonholing yourself. You may lean toward being a little of everything (a generalist) or you may focus on one (a specialist)—your answers will clue you in. I have come up with different names for these categories, based on my research, that I think are especially applicable to young adults.

The Creative   You know who you are because you can't help making things, either from scratch or by assembling something new from something that already exists. Even when you aren't actively making things, you are absorbing new ideas, new songs, new videos, new images—anything to add to your repertoire. You tend to collect things and can handle projects that are open-ended, as long as they are imaginative.

The Helper   You are the go-to person when an event, a parent, or a friend needs attention or an extra hand. You have a lot of energy to get things done, combined with a sense of social justice and empathy and your role in the larger world. Giving feels better than receiving, and it doesn't take a lot out of you to put your energy toward someone else. You like to do things that other people find valuable.

The Thinker Your mind is your playground, so you are rarely bored. You get excited about working out a problem from beginning to end and enjoy the process of learning as much as reaching the goal. Ideas and theories excite your imagination, and a conversation about a cool topic will make your day. You often come up with alternative solutions to things and turn your friends on to new concepts and trends.

The Planner Nothing pleases you more than getting stuff done, and done well, especially if you can cross it off your ever-expanding to-do lists. You excel at managing your time and, as a result, often have a lot more free time and accomplish a great deal. You like a schedule because it helps you relax to know when you need to be somewhere and it helps you have more fun after your work is done. People often turn to you to lead because you are so efficient.

The Doer You need to move your body, and you get pretty dull if you have to sit in class all day. You can accomplish whatever you set your mind to, but it is a whole lot more fun if you can use your hands and your feet too. Watching and listening just aren't your jam (and this may have given you a reputation for being easily distracted, but that's a misunderstanding). You are fully engaged when you are doing, and you need a good balance in your day between brain and muscle power.

The Communicator You are the classic people person, the hub of the social wheel. You have tons of friends and even more acquaintances, and you love to make connections between them.

You are the person everyone texts to find out what is going on or the latest gossip. You have a global approach and can see larger patterns and common ground between people. You tend to use words well and rely on them often.

Write a description of yourself that best suits you right now. If you are more of a generalist, write down the top category or two that feel right more of the time than the others:

I'm more of a _____ and a _____.

PUTTING IT TOGETHER

When you look back at your answers here and in chapter 1, you will get a very broad sense of four important motivating factors for you:

1. Where you get your energy
   (introvert or extrovert)
2. How you engage your energy internally
   (core values)
3. How you sustain your energy socially
   (communal or maestro)
4. Where you want to spend that energy
   (your interests)

Take a look at the chart on the next page, and put your finger on the row description that best suits your temperament and social preference. Then check the box (or boxes) along that row that best describes your interests right now. Once you've checked the box (or boxes), write down the motivating factors in a journal or on your core values worksheet, and as you consider different options (either in a school or as you make your alternative plans) refer back to it.

	Thinker	Planner	Communicator	Helper	Creative	Doer
Introverted/ Communal						
Extroverted/ Communal						
Introverted/ Maestro						
Extroverted/ Maestro						

Traditional Four-Year college ◄─────────────────────────► Alternative Plan

I'm asking you to do this because as you start to explore the different paths available to you as a high school graduate, you are going to go down a rabbit hole of glossy brochures and attractive websites offering you all kinds of options. It is very easy to get seduced by an idea (D1 state university? Hell, yes! Group diving with dolphins in the Gulf of Mexico? Sign me up! Field organizer for a social justice NGO? Yeah, baby!) and forget all this inner work you've just done. This can lead to a lot of disappointment later on. Does it mean you can't go to a certain school or dive with dolphins or be a grassroots volunteer? No. But you will be happier if you apply the filters you've just learned and ask more questions specific to you and your needs.

Most teens and their parents still assume or dream that college will be the first choice after high school, and there's no reason to change that assumption. However, I'm going to make the leap that if you are reading this, you have your doubts. And that doubt can take you to some pretty interesting places. Being dubious of going straight to college after graduation is actually a sign you are paying attention to the changing world, the cost of education, and your own heart. Does it mean you'll never go to college? Of course not.

What might change is your thinking around *when* you go, *where* you go, *why* you want to go, and even *how* you go (for instance,

profile

J.J. Abrams, film director

Hit movie and TV producer, director, and writer J.J. Abrams was born in New York City and raised in LA. He went to Palisades Charter High School, or Pali High, a public school that has graduated a number of famous folks. Abrams's parents were both in the "business," and he was a huge movie fan. As a teen, he got his summer dream job: he worked for Steven Spielberg, restoring some of the films the director made as a teenager. Abrams and Spielberg never met, but the experience hooked him. He got his first job writing music for a film when he was sixteen. Abrams went to Sarah Lawrence College in New York and graduated after four years with a liberal arts degree. He moved back to LA and wrote his first screenplay with a friend, Jill Mazursky. It was purchased by Touchstone Pictures and eventually became the film *Taking Care of Business*. Within a couple of years, he was writing on his own and became Hollywood's ace script fixer.

Abrams's real breakthrough came when he moved to TV and wrote the hit series *Felicity*. He moved on to *Alias* and *Lost*, and now the sky is the limit for him. Abrams was in charge of writing and producing two films in the most recent *Star Wars* trilogy. I'm guessing he's an extroverted maestro with a tendency toward being a creative, but only he can say for sure.

If you were born in 1995 or after, consider yourself a proud member of Generation Z. You are the information hounds of the new age, with untold abilities that will shape the future. You were born in a digital world, and you will grow up in an era of rapid communication, social media, and instant messaging. That means your brain is going to zoom, far surpassing the creaky gray matter of your ancestors (like me). According to *Forbes* magazine, you and others of your generation are rebels with a cause: realists who grew up in a dangerous world but are inspired to change it. Sure, we may have problems, but you would rather know them and face them than sugarcoat them. Your resilience and savvy are poised to make you some of the most capable people on the planet.

Career coach and blogger Penelope Trunk puts it this way:

> So much of the workplace today is about processing information, and Generation Z will process information at lightning speed. And the information sector will grow at twice the rate as all other jobs. We see that the more native one is to internet technology, the better one is at processing information. We can spend time lamenting the fact that people don't write essay-long memos by hand, and people don't sit at their desks uninterrupted for eight hours a day. But what is the point of the lament? It won't change. Successful leaders of the next generation will move past the lament to watching how people adapt to the change, and leveraging what happens in the workplace. Besides, the next generation will be so good at processing information that they will open doors we can only knock on today.

you might take courses online or go abroad). And in the meantime, you'll continue exploring.

What might this exploration look like? Well, if your check mark on the chart shows you tend to be an extroverted maestro with a preference for being a creative, you might be more fulfilled apprenticing at an architect's studio or volunteering for a film production company for a year before going to college. That kind of activity could help you define and refine what you want out of school and give you the life experience that separates you from the herd of other applicants. On the other hand, if you are an introverted communal with a preference for planning, you might be the perfect volunteer for an arts organization in your community, which you could do in addition to taking French online. My real goal is to get you thinking *outside* the box and more *inside* of you. To this end, I'd like you to jot down answers to these two questions in your journal or on a piece of paper and remember them as we move into planning. Heed them. Forget finding your passion—let's find your *contentment* and *meaning*.

I feel most anxious, unhappy, and pent-up when I am

_____

_____.

I feel most calm, happy, and alive when I am

_____

_____.

THE DREAM PLAN

Keeping your own personality and set of preferences, interests, and values in mind, take a few minutes to fantasize about your dream life after graduation. What would you do right after high school if absolutely nothing was in your way and all that mattered was your own happiness? If living on a fantasy island with five of your best friends and Rihanna is your dream, write it down, because that is going to tell you something (for instance, you will need a lot of money and some serious survival and construction skills). If your dream is spending four years in an elite college, strolling across ivy-clad quads, that tells you something else (you will need stellar grades, good teacher recommendations, and practice time with the SAT or ACT). Don't hold back. Who would you do it with? Where in the world would you do it? What are the qualities that would make it right for you? And how long would you want to do it for? Write it down on a separate piece of paper and store it here, because you are going to come back to this later.

Get Your Bearings

Maybe you're still deeply unsure of where all this leaves you. That's okay too! If you're still at sea, try writing down answers to the following questions:

• What do I love to do?

• What gets me out of bed in the morning and motivates me?

• What are my skills?

• What do I believe are the most important things in life (for example, closeness to family, close friendships, helping people, social justice, making money, fame)?

• What and who do I need around me to feel confident and independent (include, for instance, living situation, allowance, and electronics)?

• Where would I love to be in five years?

Making a Plan

When you are at a crossroads in life, it can feel impossible to know which road to take. In ancient times, the wrong choice meant getting lost and starving to death, or running into a passel of lions or an angry mob from a warring tribe. Today, when we come to a modern kind of crossroads, we often feel the same dread and paralysis. That's because the part of our brain that deals with fear (the amygdala) is exactly the same as it was in humans living a thousand years ago. It's known as the reptilian part of the brain because it hasn't evolved past the very basic functions that keep humans alive. In mythology, deals are made with the devil at crossroads, when most people are willing to lay down everything they have in exchange for just a little bit of certainty.

Before you go out and call up a crossroads demon, do yourself a favor and take a deep breath (and then keep reading). There is a logical way to go about making the best plan for what you should do after high school. It involves weighing your options and thoughtfully comparing the benefits and the costs of taking one path over another *before* you actually do anything.

VISUALIZATION

Okay, so you're at a crossroads. In the previous chapters, you've already done what any explorer would do in a similar situation: You've taken stock of your constitution and the tools available to you. You now have at least some inkling as to what is going to fuel you on the next leg of your journey. You've considered your basic temperament and personal preferences, and which kind of activities and social scenes are the best fit for you. You've also thought about where you would go and what you would do if you had no obstacles in your way. So we know where you're headed, and now we're going to start filling in the possible routes to that destination. But there's one more step I want you to experiment with before we get into specific options and possibilities. It's a technique called *visualization*.

Visualization is a mental rehearsal in which you imagine having or doing what you want and thinking through the various permutations of routes that will take you there. It's a tactic that's used by athletes, entrepreneurs, and executives to envision their goals so that they can achieve them more efficiently.

So, go back to your dream plan for a second and create an image in your head of what it would be like if it really happened and how you might get there. Don't worry if it sounds stupid or unattainable in real life. That's the point. If you actually knew, you wouldn't consider yourself undecided. Just close your eyes and see yourself getting to where you want to be . . .

All done? Good.

Because now it's time for a little dose of reality. I know you have what it takes to do whatever you set your mind to, but for most people that's not as easy as it sounds, no matter how amazing they may be.

If your destination is completely out of whack with the tools and fuel you have to work with at your starting point, you are going to have to adjust your expectations of what you are able to do, map out an entirely different route, or prepare yourself for some very, very hard work. Let's be honest. No matter how attached someone might get to the idea of summiting Mount Everest, it's not going to happen unless they have the constitution, the right supplies, a plan, and some help along the way. Otherwise, things are going to end badly. On Mount Everest, "badly" means freezing to death; here, closer to sea level, it's usually a bit less dramatic—but still something you want to avoid. I know it's a downer, but here's what it's going to take to get real.

PROS AND CONS WORKSHEET

As you read through the different possibilities sketched out in this book, you can use this worksheet to sketch out the real-life pros and cons of the various scenarios that appeal to you. In each section,

I will try to outline the general costs and benefits of an option that should be weighed as part of your decision, but I can't know your personal details. There may be specific reasons why one scenario works better for you than another, so it's best if you keep your own lists. This will serve two purposes: It will help you to analyze what is really important to you, and it will keep you more flexible when it comes to making your final decision. In other words, it will help you figure out what is nonnegotiable for you and what you're willing to give up.

In fact, it doesn't hurt to try out this pros and cons worksheet right now—if you have even the slightest leaning toward a certain direction, it might be worthwhile to look at the facts on paper. Take stock of your current outlook. All you need to do is create your own worksheet, modeled after this one. At the top, write out the plan of action that you're leaning toward or most concerned about (a.k.a. your "scenario"), and then make two columns: At the top of one, write "pros;" at the top of the other, write "cons." Then list out those benefits and drawbacks. Let's say you are thinking about college. Pros could be that you'll get a higher education and higher earning potential, get out of the house, and meet new friends. Cons could be that you have to split up with your significant other, take out a loan, or work with a teacher after school to help raise your grades. Go back to your core values and your interests. Does your plan reflect them? Are you challenging yourself enough? Do you feel excited by the idea of going to college?

Fill out a pros and cons worksheet for every scenario you are considering. It will be really helpful in the reality-check department.

SCENARIO: _____
_____
_____
_____

	PROS		CONS
1.			
2.			
3.			
4.			
5.			
6.			
7.			
8.			
9.			
10.			
11.			
12.			
13.			
14.			
15.			

You should be able to see right away if the pros outweigh the cons, or vice versa, just by how long the list is on each side. This is your starting point.

YOU CAN'T DO IT ALONE

At this stage of the game, the most promising course of action is probably going to require some outside help. If that's true for you, it's important to take a moment to note the people you'd need to bring on board as advisers, mentors, or aides. The most obvious ones already surround you: your parents, teachers, coaches, and friends' parents. In some cases, however, you may want professional help from people who have intimate knowledge of the industry or field you're curious about—independent college counselors, for instance, or military recruiters or even local business leaders. I'll list good databases to search; for other situations, I'll recommend asking your school guidance counselor.

In recent years, the landscape has changed so much for high school students that talking with your parents and teachers about taking time off should not be a big deal. Thank the brave undecided souls that came before you, and the education professionals who have researched and written extensively about the benefits of time off in the past few years. I've included some of them in my bibliography if you want to check them out. The bottom line is that kids who take time off between high school and college (or in between years at college) tend to have higher GPAs upon graduation from college and suffer no backlash in the job market, so parents and educational institutions have no reason to object to them. In fact, students tend to be more motivated, mature, and versatile after time off and make up for lost class credits with ease. As for those who decide to go straight into service (military, civil, or volunteer), work, or the trades, their success is tied directly with finding the right fit and livable wage and then applying themselves to the tasks at hand. It's still a good idea to have worked through the pros and cons of your plan, but don't stress too much about all the details at this stage.

Once you have read through the rest of this book and used your pros and cons worksheets, you should be able to settle on one course of action over another. This will be your preferred road map, or Plan A. Use it to present your thinking to your parents and teachers, and anyone else invested in your future, to get their buy-in. You should keep a Plan B in your pocket, and maybe even a Plan C, just in case Plan A is a nonstarter or too expensive. If you don't get buy-in, it's another reality check (and one to list as a major con). There are very few people in the world, if any, who can make lightning in a bottle all by themselves.

EXECUTING YOUR PLAN

Because planning for big life events and goals is complex and time-consuming, it is helpful to take a step back and consider what the execution of a plan means. Whether you're just getting started or want to do a kind of status check, the following steps represent a fair picture of what a plan in action requires from you, in real terms.

These are the steps—but how they are taken is entirely up to you.

PORTRAIT OF A PLAN IN ACTION

1. You commit to the plan, after weighing pros and cons.
2. You obtain all the necessary information about aspects of your plan (whether via internet, a library, a bookstore, or an agency or organization).
3. You talk to your parents and any other adults who may have insights and advice to offer (or who simply need to approve the given plan), especially if they are helping support you financially.
4. You create a timeline and checklist for action points.
5. You review your budget in light of expected costs and discuss it with people who are invested.
6. You take action—delivering all necessary paperwork and deposits on time.
7. You make life/work/travel plans and housing arrangements.
8. You wrap up loose ends.

A PLAN IN ACTION

Let's say, for instance, that a common thread in your activities list is building things and using your hands. Maybe you think that learning carpentry skills could be a good way to support yourself. You might also like the idea of being able to build your own house someday, maybe even designing it, maybe even becoming an architect—but for right now, given what you have to work with (your starting point), carpentry seems like a good scenario. What next?

Take out your pros and cons worksheet and put "Carpentry" at the top. Then list the first pros and cons that come to mind. If, after looking at the initial pros and cons (there may be more to add as you move along in the process), the scenario still seems pretty good, commit to the idea. Start researching journeymen certification programs in carpentry by going online, asking your school guidance counselor, or both. There may be a good trade school near you that fits the bill (see chapter 8 for more specifics) and allows you to live at home (better on the budget) or an online course that will help you get started. Once you have specific information, print it out and talk over the options with your parents. The information should be as detailed as you can make it. You'll want to know exactly what you might be signing up for, such as buying necessary tools and supplies, program fees, workshop space, how many hours it takes to get a certification (a must if you want to subcontract for other people), and what kinds of apprenticeship opportunities, skills, or portfolio you will have at the end of the program.

If your parents and advisers accept your plan, discuss your needs and specific schedule. Ask your parents how they would like to handle the living arrangements and what they might expect you to pay for. Remember, you are an adult now, and the free ride is turning into a semi-free one. We'll talk at length about budget in the next chapter, which will help you estimate how doable your plan is financially. Once you have an idea of how much you can afford, it's time to fill out the application and make your deposit. In the time remaining before the program starts, you'll need to assemble the necessary gear, get the appropriate materials and space to work with, and clear your schedule of other obligations so you can focus on building your new skill. If your budget is dependent on your getting a part-time job to pay for your program, you should take this time to get that going.

WHAT IF YOU CHANGE YOUR MIND?

Changing your mind is your prerogative and should only be an issue if you have enlisted in the military or have laid down some fat stacks in a deposit that you can't get back (be careful of this, especially with online courses and travel abroad programs). If you aren't sure about a choice, you might be able to try it out first by taking a summer course or night class. If you can't transfer or drop the plan without big penalties (or, in the case of the military, possible prosecution), you need to dig deep and persevere. There was a reason you thought this plan might be good, so go back to that. Hold that in your mind, and work hard to get what you can out of the program. And recognize that sometimes we don't know what skills will be useful later on.

But if something is *really* not right, and you know it in your bones, no amount of money, time, or perseverance is going to make it right. In this case, you will have to figure out a way to exit gracefully. Often this will require you to present an alternative plan—and it should be really tight. You will have eaten up some of your credibility with your folks, but you should be able to earn it back if you have clear reasons why plan A is not working out and why plan B has the potential to last. And it goes without saying— but I'll say it anyway—that you should not stick to a plan if you are being mentally, physically, or financially abused or discriminated against by the people in control.

KEEPING IT REAL

Any plan you make—tentative or actual—should address the following basic questions:

What?	College, service, work, travel, independent study, time off, hybrid
Where?	Local, national, international, hybrid
Who?	Kind of institution, program, business, organization, or self-guided
When?	Time span
Why?	Education, self-improvement, self-knowledge, skill training, stress relief, strength building, self-invention, professional or educational development, cross-cultural literacy, language development, personal growth
How?	Potential wage, stipend, loan, or other financial support; travel; transportation; living situation; health care

TALKING TO YOUR PARENTS

Regardless of how trendy taking time off has become, for some of you it is still a hard thing to have a conversation about, let alone implement. The more traditional or restrictive your family culture is, the stickier it will be to do something unexpected—especially if you are the first one in your family to have a chance to go to college. Only you know what the culture of your family is and how well your plan is going to be received. Only you know the history of communication styles in your family. It may feel like the path of least resistance to go along just to get along (that is, to enter a premed program because your parents are both doctors or to forget your dream of becoming a dancer because your parents find it unrealistic), but if every instinct is telling you to do something different, pay attention to your gut.

looking back

"It took me three years of college in a pre-nursing program before I realized I had absolutely no desire to be a nurse. None. My parents really wanted me to be a nurse, and there was a lot of expectation put on me to finish the program. I was never interested in studying, although for some reason I managed to do okay in high school. I liked physics a lot because the teacher and I shared a mutual love of reggae, but aside from that, I had no drive for academics. What I did have was a passion for the idea of travel, and I dreamt that someday I would have a job that would take me all over the world, but at that time it was like wishing I had a job that would take me to the moon. It wasn't possible. What was possible was a good job in nursing. So I ignored my true heart's leanings and dutifully applied and got into the local university. My junior year we started our clinical rotations, and I couldn't bear it anymore. I was miserable. I took some time off, returned briefly to try to get a degree in biology, and found myself at the library studying maps of India and China instead of physiology. Finally, it dawned on me that what I really wanted to do was social work, preferably in a foreign country. Once that clicked, my path was clear—at least to me. My parents took some convincing. It took me several years and a lot of grief to figure out what I really wanted to do, but it was totally worth it."

—J. Mills, founder and executive director,
Limitless Child International

Many people reach middle age only to freak out because they finally come to terms with the fact that they've been living somebody else's idea of a life—usually with a script written by their parents' expectations. That's why you'll find so many forty- and fifty-somethings getting divorced, learning how to skydive, quitting their jobs, and generally doing what they should have done back when they were your age. I'd like to save you the freak-out and have you do what you really want to do now, when you have fewer responsibilities, more time, and more energy. If it feels hard to talk to your parents now, think about how it might feel someday to talk to your spouse, kids, or employer and announce that you are leaving your life behind to go and find yourself.

If you've sketched out a plan and begun to narrow in on specifics, you have already made it a lot harder for your parents—or anyone else—to doubt you. They may have legitimate concerns at this point—and you should absolutely give them a chance to air those grievances. If they do, pay attention! Your parents have known you for your entire life, and they may have some insights or ideas that you didn't think of yourself. Moreover, it will be much easier for you emotionally, and far easier financially, if they can assist you a little—by funding your plan outright or by helping you get aid or other kinds of financing, such as a bank loan.

If your parents are still dead set against your plan, for whatever reasons, enlist the help of another relative or a teacher or counselor to mediate your conversations. Go over the pros and cons step-by-step so your parents can understand your thinking. Try to be understanding of their point of view and life experience. If you don't mind compromising, see where along the way you could do this without sacrificing your dream.

If all else fails, and if the walls of resistance fail to crumble before your dream, work around those barriers. Respectfully agree to disagree and go after alternative forms of support. Appeal to your guidance counselor at school. Find scholarship opportunities (see page 83 to get started). Reach out to a teacher or another adult you can trust and ask for advice. At age eighteen, you will be legally considered an adult and can make your own way. In the end, if you are happy and can support yourself, your parents will come around eventually.

looking back

"I have dyslexia, so getting through school took a lot of brain power and focus for me. I was totally burnt out by high school graduation, and I knew I didn't want to go to college. My parents kept telling me that I needed more education to get a good job, so I went anyway. I only lasted a month. I spent the next three years out on my own, working, paying my own bills, getting by. Then the lightbulb went off. I suddenly wanted to get more education, so I went back to college and successfully got my degree, all on my own."

—C. Smith, lab technician

Money Matters

Hands down, lack of funds is the biggest bummer when planning life after high school. If money were no object, only lack of imagination, grades, test scores, and family expectations would get in the way of doing what you want to do after graduation. Unfortunately, money *is* an object. A big one. For most high school seniors and their parents, it's the stratospheric cost of college that causes a reevaluation of what is possible. Even if you don't go straight to college, you will still need money. The only question is *how much* you will need. Does this mean if you have no money, you can't do anything but shelve your dreams and get a menial job? A resounding *no*! Thankfully, you have a ton of options—and I'm not just talking about a handout from your parents or relatives (although that can certainly help). Because of your age and your individual promise, financial aid, scholarships, fellowships, military benefits, work-study programs, friendly investors, and day wages are all possible contributors. You just have to look at your plan and consider your options. You might have to mix it up a little by combining funding sources (for example: parental sponsorship, a gift from Uncle Joe, a scholarship, and a part-time dishwashing job) to reach your goal, but it is doable—and infinitely more so if you are specific about how much you think you need and what you want to spend it on. So let's break it down.

LIVING COSTS

First things first: Let's find out what it will cost you to live in the early 21st century on your own, whether you travel, work, start a business, volunteer, or hang out and record your first album. These are baseline expenses, so remember that educational costs are extra! From where you are sitting now, it might be hard to estimate these costs, but give it a shot. Ask for help from your folks too. If you have no idea what rent might be, use the local online classified ads or Craigslist listings as a guide—or you might consider speaking with a local real estate agent. Look at rental ads for studio or shared apartments, and plug in that number as your estimate. These numbers are not real quite yet—you are simply trying to get a basic idea of living expenses. On the following pages is a budget worksheet that will help you start working out the details.

Once you add up everything, you may find you can't afford to live on your own—and even that is useful (if disappointing) information.

You can also use this sheet to help estimate your personal annual expenses if you decide to apply for financial aid to go to college (but if that's the case, remember to subtract room, food, and utilities).

MONTHLY INCOME	GROSS	NET
Allowance (Family Support)	$	$
Job	$	$
Student Loans	$	$
Other	$	$
Total	$	$

MONTHLY EXPENSES	CURRENT	PROPOSED
Rent/Mortgage	$	$
Utilities	$	$
Cell Phone	$	$
TV and Internet	$	$
Groceries	$	$
Health/Dental Insurance	$	$
Prescriptions/Doctor Visits	$	$
Auto Payments/Registration	$	$
Auto Insurance/Maintenance/Repair	$	$
Gas	$	$
Parking/Tolls/Public Transportation	$	$
Laundry/Dry Cleaning	$	$
Salon/Barber/Self Care	$	$
Movies/Music	$	$
Dining Out/Takeout	$	$
Vacation/Travel	$	$

Books/Subscriptions	$	$
Gym/Club Membership	$	$
Hobbies/Personal	$	$
Clothing	$	$
Loan/Credit Card Payments	$	$
Bank Fees/Postage/Stationery	$	$
Charitable Donations	$	$
Savings	$	$
Other	$	$
Total	**$**	**$**

HARD TRUTH		
Total Net Income	$	$
Total Monthly Expenses	$	$
Monthly Surplus or Overdraw	**$**	**$**

EDUCATIONAL COSTS

College graduates are predicted to have an income about 83 percent
higher over their life spans than people who do not have a college
degree. That's a lot of cheddar, I know, but it doesn't come without
a hefty upfront investment. According to the College Board's 2018
Trends in College Pricing report, the *average* total annual sticker price for
2018-2019 (including tuition, fees, books, supplies, housing, and other
expenses including transportation) of a two-year public college for
commuting students renting a living space was $17,930. For a four-year
public college or university, the average annual cost for on-campus
students was $25,890 for in state and $41,950 for out of state. It was a
whopping average of $52,500 for students living on campus at a
four-year nonprofit private college or university. For the most selective

and elite schools? A jaw-dropping average of $72,000 annually! In 2019 the most expensive college in the US was Harvey Mudd, a West Coast Ivy League school, ringing in at a grand total of $75,003.

Dollar amounts of academic grants and financial aid awards have also risen to help offset costs, and each student will have their individual need assessed based on their family's financial profile. Many of the most competitive private institutions boast that they are "need blind" and will help any student, once accepted, to foot the bill. At Princeton the average aid award package is around $53,572, or two-thirds the cost of going (once you factor in room and board and all the other expenses). However, even at these levels, student aid is not keeping up with the rising price of a college education, and many folks are turning to private loans to make up the difference.

Table represents average annual costs of attending college, including tuition, fees, room and board, books, supplies and other expenses:

TYPE OF COLLEGE/LIVING SITUATION	AVERAGE ANNUAL COST
Two-year public college for commuting students not living at home	$17,930
Four-year public college or university for in-state students living on campus	$25,890
Four-year public college or university for out-of-state students living on campus	$41,950
Four-year private college or university	$52,500
Four-year most selective private college or university	$72,000

Colleges, universities, and private study programs—be they two or four years, whether here, overseas, or online—have the same categories of basic annual living expenses. The total will vary widely depending on where you go, where you live, what you want to study, and for how long. When calculating costs, start with the maximum and then figure out where there's wiggle room. (For example, maybe you can go to an in-state school, rent a room off campus that's cheaper than the dorms, or do a program in Vietnam instead of Paris.) Apples to apples, the cost of an in-state public college is about 73 percent less than a private college, and it's not the worst idea to ask yourself if your in-state university system offers an education that is 73 percent worse than a private, elite school. Sure it might not have the cachet, but that is a huge amount of money that could be saved (or not borrowed).

Anyway, more on that in a moment. For planning purposes, use these numbers as a base in your calculations.

NET PRICE AND LOAN CALCULATORS—USE THEM!

At bigfuture.collegeboard.org you will find different calculators that will help you estimate the cost of college, and the estimated cost of any loans you might take, including the Federal Direct Student Loan and any private loans. I tried out the student loan calculator using an estimated starting salary of $35,000 and a loan amount of $37,000, or $8,000 per year for four years, with an interest rate of 6.5 percent. My results indicated that, factoring in interest (a startling $8,991!), I would owe $45,991 in principal and interest upon graduation and owe a combined monthly payment of $383 if I planned to pay off the loan in ten years, or 12 percent of my income. A $35,000 per year salary minus taxes pays $2,500 a month, so after student loan payments, I would have $2,117 to pay for rent, food, car, gas, phone, and other bills. In the US, the average rent in 2019 was $1,465 . . . so you can see how easy it is to get underwater with loans. Standard wisdom is that your monthly student debt load should not exceed 12 to 15 percent of your projected monthly income (as if you know that amount now). My wisdom says the less debt the better and no debt is the best. In fact, unless you get into an Ivy or an equivalent "name" college that brings a big scholarship and a lot of Old World prestige with your diploma, my advice is to go to a cheaper, lesser-known college, pay half the price, and *stay out of debt*.

WHAT ARE YOU PAYING FOR?

Tuition and Fees. Tuition is the cost of instructing you for a year (fall to spring) at the institution or program you want to be a part of. Fees are standard additional costs, such as for library and computer use, ID cards, social activities, parking, lab or studio access, diploma, and graduation. They are all considered part of the academic experience, but not part of the actual instruction. Tuition and fees are usually lumped together for estimation purposes. Annual tuition and fees at specific schools are pretty easy to find because most institutions have a website that explains the fee structure in detail. Just for kicks, I recommend getting numbers from four different kinds of schools: an in-state public university, a private college or university, an out-of-state public university, and your local community college. It is interesting to see the difference. Note (again!) that going to a private four-year college is often much more expensive than attending an in-state four-year school.

Room and Board. This is what it costs to keep a roof over your head and food in your belly for the academic year—if you live on

When you estimate the cost of tuition, keep in mind that some programs have a per-credit-hour rate that is charged by the semester. If money is going to be tight, and you don't want to take on debt, you could decide to take fewer classes per semester and graduate in five or six years, instead of four, which will free up some time to work and save while you study.

campus or on-site and eat on a meal plan. According to the College Board, the average cost of room and board in 2018-2019 ranged from $11,140 at four-year public schools to $12,680 at four-year private schools. Some institutions break out housing and meal expenses, while others keep them together. The most up-to-date yearly expenses can be found on individual websites. But there is a lot of wiggle room here. You can live off campus and eat at school or, better yet, live at home and pack your lunch. Still, for planning purposes, estimate the maximum and then adjust.

Books and Supplies. This is often a surprise expense because textbooks are costly! Most colleges will publish the average costs for required books and supplies. Additional supplies include printed class materials, required reading materials, reference books, and the usual pens, pencils, and notebooks. Depending on the program, lab supplies or computer and copy charges may be lumped in. The College Board reported that the average cost for buying books and supplies for 2018-2019 was about $1,400—a good enough estimate to use for now.

Personal Expenses/Transportation. Go back to your budget worksheet to estimate your miscellaneous expenses without room and board or any of the attending costs, like utilities. Don't forget things like seasonal clothing, dorm room necessities (like bed linen), parking, transportation, laundry, cell phone, entertainment, and any splurges, like concert tickets, beer, or a fancy meal out, and add this number to your total. You may be surprised at how much these extras cost, even if you are living in campus housing. Don't forget the cost of travel home if you are applying to schools far away.

KIND	ANNUAL ESTIMATED COST
Tuition and Program Fees	$
Room and Board	$
Books and Supplies	$
Personal Expenses/Transportation	$
Other	$
Total	$

Do you have sticker shock? I don't blame you. It's pretty mindboggling to look at the bottom line of higher education—and I hope that this country comes to its senses soon because these stratospheric costs are becoming unsustainable for all but the very, very wealthy.

FEDERAL STUDENT LOANS

Once upon a time, educational loans were like any other loan—a car loan or a bank loan, requiring the kind of credit and financial picture a majority of young people don't have. Prizing the value of an educated populace, the federal government tried to make higher education more accessible to all young people in 1965 by guaranteeing educational loans from private lenders to loosen up the eligibility requirements. This was called the Family Financial Education Loan (FFEL) Program. Congress changed the law in 1990 to allow the federal government to provide direct student loans (no third-party lender) that require no credit check or cosigner. It changed again in 2010, when FFEL was eliminated, and the Direct Loan Program was enacted. This move was made with good intentions (to make postsecondary education available to everyone, regardless of financial status), but a number of unintended consequences followed, including but not limited to ballooning tuition prices, stagnant wages, a shift in employment trends to lower-income jobs, predatory lenders, and an alarming rate of loan defaults. Confusion about payment terms and the Student Loan Forgiveness Program hasn't helped, nor has the involvement of government-contracted third-party "loan servicers," whose practices are often obscure and difficult to oversee. Add to this that student loans are pooled, traded, and sold to investors as commodities on Wall Street (student loan asset-backed securities, or SLABS), and you have a situation where one person's debt is another person's windfall. Like medical debt, federal student loan debt has created its own industrial complex, with many fat-cat players seated at the table, dining out on your desire to get educated.

Federal loans are a completely different animal than merit grants or scholarships (which are, essentially, gifts; they do not have to be repaid), or work-study programs (in which you exchange your labor for a reduction in cost), but colleges and universities present these loans as part of your overall financial aid package. This can be misleading, so pay attention. At the beginning of each academic year, you will be notified of your eligibility for federal loans, along with the amount you are eligible for. This happens as a matter of course on your tuition bill if you have filled out the FAFSA (see page 76). The bill will give you a breakdown of the full cost of the semester, minus any merit or academic grants or scholarships, minus the federal financial loans (subsidized and unsubsidized), and then

💡 Federal Student Loan Breakdown

There are a number of different kinds of federal loans. Some are subsidized (based on need), and some are unsubsidized (available to anyone regardless of need).

Direct subsidized loans are made to eligible undergraduate students who demonstrate financial need, to help cover the costs of higher education at a college or career school.

Direct unsubsidized loans are made to eligible undergraduate, graduate, and professional students, but eligibility is not based on financial need.

Direct PLUS loans are made to graduate or professional students and parents of dependent undergraduate students to help pay for education expenses not covered by other financial aid. Eligibility is not based on financial need, but a credit check is required. Borrowers who have an adverse credit history must meet additional requirements to qualify.

Direct consolidation loans allow you to combine all of your eligible federal student loans into a single loan with a single loan servicer.

calculate your net cost at the bottom. If you sign the letter, you are agreeing to take on the loans, with interest. And these loans do not go away if you declare bankruptcy unless you can prove "undue hardship" on your dependents. This is almost impossible to do. If you die, the government will currently discharge your federal loans (Sweet! But, oh yeah, you are dead). Most private student loans don't even give you that relief because they transfer the load onto your survivors, and divorce won't save you either. In fact, if someday you marry someone with a ton of student debt, you just might become liable for it too.

Think of student loan debt as a chain you will have to carry around for a certain amount of time. The weight and length of it depends on your choices. If you want to steer clear of the federal direct loans, you must opt out of taking federal aid when you sign your tuition commitment letter. Many kids simply sign the paper, focusing only on the net cost at the bottom, and unwittingly take on the loans without thinking about or even checking the terms of repayment. They only realize they've taken on the loans when they get a bill the following month for the first payment (or, if they have a subsidized loan, after the grace period ends). Colleges don't make this clearer because, honestly, including the loans on the tuition bill makes their costs look lower. In reality, you will be paying more over time because all these loans charge fees and interest.

THE PROBLEM WITH DEBT

Taking on debt is a scary proposition, and one I am going to caution you about over and over again. However, there is such a thing as reasonable debt that serves your potential. Graduating with a BA and $15,000–$20,000 worth of total debt is reasonable (by total, I also mean credit cards and car payments!) because there is a high likelihood you will be able to earn enough income to pay it back in a reasonable amount of time, even if you choose a lower-paying profession. Not everyone can be a hedge fund broker, no matter what your parents imagine.

FAFSA

If you're beginning the process of figuring out how to pay for college, you've probably heard or seen this mysterious acronym before. Guidance counselors, teachers, friends, and the internet use FAFSA when talking about paying for school. But what does it mean? What is it?

Well, FAFSA stands for the Free Application for Federal Student Aid. This form, which can be found and completed online at FAFSA.ed.gov, is the means by which you become eligible for federal student loans, grants, and work-study jobs. Completing FAFSA is the first step toward gaining access to the nearly $185 billion available in federal, state, college, and private funds.

An incredible amount of information is out there on everything FAFSA related, whether that's how to fill it out and when to file (hint: as early as possible!) or accounts of others' experiences with it. Here are a few places to start looking:

- bigfuture.collegeboard.org/pay-for-college/financial-aid
- studentaid.ed.gov
- studentaid.ed.gov/fafsa

Graduating with $50,000–$75,000 in debt for a BA is not prudent, unless you are darn sure you will walk out of school with skills and opportunities to land a job that will make you a bundle right off the bat.

As you research taking on loans (either for college or for any post-high school plan), know that the picture changes rapidly. Media reports regularly address what is going on with the student loan debt apocalypse, and things are so in flux that what I write today probably will be out of date by the time you read this. Such is the case when student debt is increasing by $170,000 a minute and people are defaulting on their loans at such a scary rate that talk of a national loan forgiveness plan is gaining in popularity. Even so, it is important to understand why taking on debt, even for a great thing like higher education, is such a huge and potentially devastating calamity for your personal financial picture and our national economy.

There are two kinds of debt: good debt and bad debt. Good debt is money you borrow for a specific amount of time to help you do something that will allow you to pay the money back in that time span (a return on investment) and help you move on to bigger and better things as well. Let's say you want to take a two-week trip to South Dakota and volunteer to help a team of vets spay and neuter stray puppies. You borrow $3,000 for airfare, accommodations, food, and a rental car. You spend two weeks assisting, and when you get back, one of the vets hires you for the summer as a full-time vet tech and pays you twenty dollars an hour. You work for eight weeks and (pretax) make $6,400. Depending on your tax rate, you likely end up with around $5,800, which allows you to pay back the initial loan and interest in full and still come out with approximately $2,500 and a summer learning valuable skills that you can build on. In this scenario, the debt acts in a very real sense as seed money.

Bad debt includes credit card debt. It goes to fund a purchase or a lifestyle choice that is unlikely to reap enough of a return to make the required payments and eventually clear the debt. Both kinds roll over and can go into default if you don't make regular payments, which can wreck your credit and trigger bankruptcy. For much of this country's history, educational debt was considered good debt, but that's not necessarily the case anymore.

Since 1989 the cost of college has spiked 129 percent. Scarily, the price of college now increases twice as fast as the rate of inflation. Inflation marks the increase in the cost of living and is the reason why a bus fare in 2019 costs $2.75 but was only 75 cents twenty years ago even though the bus is driving the same route. (The same thing goes for the cost of a slice of pizza or a cup of coffee over roughly the same period.) Nicer buses, higher gas prices, bus driver pay raises, and changes in the value of the dollar all contribute to that rise, and other commodities and services experience comparable increases. Except for colleges and universities. Their prices are totally out of whack with what people can afford. According to *Forbes*, the price of college is outpacing wage growth at a staggering rate. As of 2016, a person would have to work eight times as many hours as someone in 1989 to pay for the same amount of education.

No wonder two-thirds of college students and grads (even not-so-recent grads) are shackled by debt and the inability to get a job with a high enough salary to pay off that debt (and that doesn't even include credit card debt). The other reason is interest on that debt. According to a 2019 report by Student Loan Hero, the average loan debt per college student is $39,400.

Interest rates on federal student loans fluctuate every year: In 2017-2018, the interest rate was 4.45 percent. In 2018-2019, it was 4.53 percent for subsidized loans, 6.08 percent for unsubsidized loans, and 7.08 percent for Direct PLUS, and it will likely change again next year. Added to this is a "loan fee" that usually hovers around 1 percent but can be as high as 4 or 5 percent! These rates can cause loans to balloon, especially those for grad school and professional schools, so that repaying that debt becomes like digging a hole that just refills with sand. For example, if you had the average student direct subsidized loan balance of $39,400 with a 5.05 percent interest rate and a $419 monthly payment, you'd pay over $10,000 in interest fees over ten years and end up having to pay back more than $50,000. I cannot emphasize this enough: borrowed money is not free. For every dollar you borrow, you might have to pay back a *minimum* of $1.05 (based on this year's rates). Only you know your financial situation, so my best advice is to talk to your parents or guardian and fully understand the kind of loan you are considering, the interest rate you might be expected to pay over the course of the repayment, how this breaks down compared to your potential ability to earn, and whether or not you can rely on help from your parents to repay your loans. Based on these numbers alone, direct subsidized loans are better debt than unsubsidized or PLUS loans, so pay attention not only to how much you qualify for but what *kind* of loan it is.

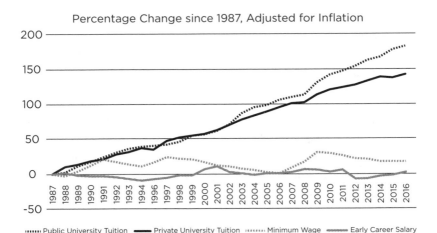

Percentage Change since 1987, Adjusted for Inflation

⋯⋯ Public University Tuition ▬▬ Private University Tuition ⋯⋯ Minimum Wage ▬▬ Early Career Salary

When you borrow money, you are borrowing the amount you need (say $10,000). This is considered the principal. You will also pay the interest rate (for easy math sake, let's say 5 percent). Most loans are conventional principal/interest loans, which means that every payment you make gets split to pay interest first and then part of the principal, eventually eliminating the debt over a set amount of time. Some loans are interest-only loans and offer lower monthly payments that temporarily pay off interest for a five- to ten-year window, after which you will either have to convert the loan to a higher monthly payment conventional principal and interest loan or pay a balloon payment on your principal. This can be catastrophic for your finances if you don't have thousands of dollars stashed away, so keep it simple and stay away from interest-only loans.

The bottom line: Take on as little debt as possible to pay for your education—even if this means taking more time to get your degree and working. Or going to a state school instead of a private college. And don't rely on the Federal Student Loan Forgiveness Program, because, as of this writing, 99 percent of claims are rejected.

If you do get a loan, read your contract carefully and understand whether the loan is an interest-only loan (Stop! Don't sign!) or a principal and interest loan. Have the terms of repayment explained to you, and carefully consider if the profession you are studying for will pay you enough to repay the loan. As I'm writing this, because of the student debt problem, many people are being discouraged from going into the liberal arts. But the world needs

English and history majors as much as business and health policy majors, so don't give up on your dream . . . just be careful how you finance it.

Also, remember that your debt must be paid whether or not you graduate (Which is the point, right? Degree = higher income). If you take on debt, be prepared to go all the way and get that degree. If you drop or fail out, you will still have to pay your debt.

OTHER WAYS TO PAY

Expected Family Contribution

This is a fancy name for something super simple: how much money the government or a certain institution calculates that you and your parents can afford to contribute toward your education. It is the number your family is "expected" to pay, not necessarily what they can afford or what they will eventually contribute (the real contribution is highly dependent on individual institutions and the packages they will offer you). Financial aid rubrics vary from institution to institution, but all use the same basic numbers to figure out how much assistance you will need. The formula takes into account all of your family's assets, the taxes they pay, and the value of real estate holdings (not including your house). Some calculators even include your siblings' assets! To estimate what your family contribution might be, you can go to the College Board website, bigfuture.collegeboard.org, and walk through the Board's calculator. When you fill out the FAFSA, your expected family contribution will be calculated for you as well.

Scholarships and Grants

If you have talent, drive, and stellar grades, you can probably get a scholarship to help you pay for school. There are thousands out there, and some aren't academia based. Scholarships are awarded to people who come from a certain state, are immigrants, or are a certain ethnicity. There are also grants for artists, for tinkerers, for community service, for environmental stewardship—or for the kids of parents who work in a particular field. The two things they all have in common are eligibility requirements and the need for a candidate to have a distinguished record. Many of these one-of-a-kind scholarships are school or organization specific. Listed below are databases where you can start your search. A word to the wise, however: most of these databases have been scooped up by education lenders, so by giving them your information you will become part of their lending database and you may receive some spam as a result.

Here are some general scholarship databases:

- College Board Scholarship Search: bigfuture.collegeboard.org /scholarship-search
- Fastweb: fastweb.com
- Peterson's: petersons.com
- Scholarships.com: scholarships.com/about-us
- CollegeNET: collegenet.com
- Cappex: cappex.com

If you already have an idea of what school or schools you want to attend, call up the financial aid offices and ask about additional scholarships you can apply for. You'll be surprised by how willing admissions officers and financial aid folks are to help. You'll be even more surprised by what other opportunities you'll learn about. A great many of these school-based scholarships are partial and won't cover the entire annual cost of attending their school. So keep in mind all the expenses we've covered and don't get seduced by what may seem like a great offer.

Crunch the numbers (all of them), and then look at what is being offered. Like I said, if you need to take out a modest federal direct student loan to cover the rest (like $2,000–$4,000 per year), then you should be okay. If you have to go much higher than that, you might need to reconsider.

And, finally, ask your parents to check with the human resources departments at their jobs about scholarships. Many companies have grants or scholarship programs for the children of employees. Here are a few companies that offer these opportunities:

- Siemens. If your parents work for this conglomerate, you may be in luck—you could be eligible for a $4,000 scholarship.
- Intel. The computer giant gives out $1.4 million in scholarships every year to the children of its employees.
- US government. As the child of a federal employee, and thanks to the fine people at the Federal Employee Education and Assistance Fund, you can apply for $500 to $5,000 to help pay for school.
- Fluor. This engineering and construction corporation offers one-time and renewable scholarships.

Instruction and program fees and travel and transportation costs
will be relevant to nonacademic programs you might be interested
in. Many (but not all) independent study, volunteer, and internship
programs have scholarships that can reduce fees for qualified
participants. Compare and contrast pricing when you look at the
individual sites for these programs.

FINANCING THE ALTERNATIVE DREAM

What about those of you who are thinking about not going to
college right away, if ever? The good news on the financial front
is that you will have all the time in the world to work and make
money—if you can find a job. Your chances of doing just that
increase the more education you get, as will your income (see page
96). If you already have a job, you may be able to expand your
hours or trade up to a better position or salary once you graduate.
I encourage you to set a goal for yourself and work toward it.
Your work will be much more meaningful if it's part of a larger
investment in yourself and your dreams.

If you are saving to finance the dream, living at home and cutting
back on spending will help significantly. If your parents know what
your goal is and that the current situation is temporary, subsidizing
you with free rent and board as you make money won't be as much
of an issue. But if it is, remind them how much education costs
today. Money saved is money earned, right?

If you have a business that you want to start right away, you may need an adult with proven credit to cosign a bank loan or give you a personal loan. You will have to set out your financial projections in a business plan (for more on this, see chapter 16), which will help both parties understand their obligations and rewards. Starting a business is financially risky and takes time, so be prepared to keep your expenses very low and work or intern somewhere in the meantime.

FINANCIAL WORKSHEET

We've gone over a lot of numbers, I know, but let's try to wrap it all up in a tidy package that gives you a bottom line to work with as you plan. Use this worksheet to combine all the possible sources of income you might receive after graduating and all the possible expenses, totaled from all the worksheets. These numbers can be based on annual or monthly income and expenditures.

INCOME	ANNUAL/MONTHLY
Expected Family Contribution	$
Scholarships/Grants/Work Study	$
Student Loans	$
Job/Wages	$
Personal Gifts	$
Other	+ $
Subtotal	$
Total Expenses	- $
Total (The Bottom Line)	= $

WHERE THE RUBBER HITS THE ROAD

In the final analysis, money is potential and you can invest whatever funds you have in many different scenarios. In the world we live in now, there is no guarantee that a college degree is going to land you a solid job with a paycheck and benefits the way it once did. Currently, the pressure to "make good" is largely being placed on a loose ideal of "personal responsibility"; as in, if you take out $30,000 in debt to go to college and major in philosophy, you only have yourself to blame. Why didn't you get a degree in systems engineering? This is a simplistic idea that does a disservice not only to philosophy majors but to all of humanity and the society that we have built on the back of a classic liberal arts education. The world needs English and sociology and art history majors as much as they need hospitality, sports psychology, and marketing majors. But since we have

profile

Barack Obama II, 44th US president

President Obama was born in 1961 in Honolulu, Hawaii. His mother, Ann Dunham, grew up in Kansas. His father, Barack Obama Sr., was born in Kenya, Africa, and he earned a scholarship that allowed him to move to Hawaii to study, where he met and married Dunham. The couple divorced when Barack was only two, and Obama Sr. had no contact with his son. A couple of years later, Dunham remarried and the family moved to Indonesia, where Barack's stepfather was from. Barack was ten years old when his mother sent him back to Hawaii to live with her parents, where he would be educated and safe from the civil unrest she witnessed in Indonesia. He was elected president of the United States in 2008 and inaugurated in 2009. Obama is the first truly multicultural president: white, black, American, African, and Indonesian. He did not grow up with much money and relied on scholarships, loans, and contributions from his family to fund his education.

In the fifth grade, Obama attended an elite private school in Hawaii, thanks to a scholarship. He was an excellent student, but writes in his books, *The Audacity of Hope* and *Dreams from My Father*, that he struggled to find his social identity (and come to terms with his father abandoning him) as one of only three African Americans at his school. During high school, Obama won a scholarship to study at Occidental College in Los Angeles, where he stayed for two years (with financial aid from his grandparents). He then transferred to Columbia University and took out student loans. He graduated in 1983 with a degree in political science and went on to get his law degree from Harvard University in 1991. After working on the white-collar side of things for two years, Obama moved to Chicago's South Side and took a job as a community organizer before being elected to Congress. The rest, as they say, is history.

to live in the real world where no one is doing us any favors, I will end with this: you can be anything you want to be, but you might have to get creative in where you go, how you fund it, and how long it takes.

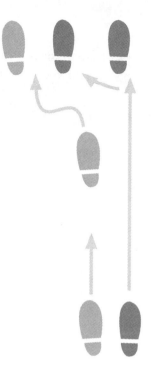

Education breeds confidence.
Confidence breeds hope.
Hope breeds peace.

—*Confucius*

part two:

higher education

What You Need to Know

You've taken stock of your past and thought a bit about your future, and now it's time to start considering, in detail, some of those unknown lands we talked about earlier. But we are going to move slowly and start with something you already know a fair amount about: school. Besides all the practical arguments for going to college after you graduate, there are some that are just as important but only rarely discussed. College, or any advanced learning institution, is a relatively safe bet. A diploma or a certificate will serve you well in life, and the process of attaining it can also provide many valuable lessons (about how to navigate complicated procedures, submit important paperwork in a timely fashion, and generally just get things done). School offers a familiar environment: teachers, class schedules, a ready-made group of peers, cafeterias, homework, and regular vacations.

And within that familiar framework you have a once-in-a-lifetime chance to try on a wide spectrum of future possibilities with very little risk.

If you are enrolled as a student and take the required prerequisites, a good college can become the best sampling board around, offering an amazing array of courses from French Philosophers of the Eighteenth Century to Cellular Biology to Broadcast News 101. The facilities aren't a bad perk either, as even schools with smaller endowments come replete with beautiful libraries, huge swimming pools, and coffee bars aplenty. And never again will you have the same opportunity to make friends with so many people your same age (who happen to be going through exactly the same experience at the exact same time). These are the kinds of friendships that can last forever. Life may never be as mind expanding or as cushy or as downright fun as the years spent as an undergraduate. However, as we discovered in the last section, those years come with a hefty price tag, which opens the discussion to an important question: Is more school really necessary?

I know the arguments against it. They run something like this: You're already burnt out. You've had enough of sitting in a classroom. You've already accomplished a lot in high school— enough to get the only kind of early-life jobs, at least, that the economy is offering these days. (No one needs a degree to work at American Eagle.) You could go out and make money now. Do something real. Look at somebody like Bill Gates. He didn't graduate from college. Neither did Steve Jobs or Mark Zuckerberg or Ben Affleck or Natalie Portman. They're doing fine, right? School is ridiculously expensive. It's hard to get in anyway. Education is moving online, so why all the grief?

YEAH, WHY ALL THE GRIEF?

It's a common complaint—especially from the often very talented people who succeeded despite their lack of a college education. College is so pricey, and college life, for many kids, leaves so much to be desired (pressure drinking, sexual harassment, loneliness, crappy food, crowded courses, gross dorms, etc.) that the real-world value of an undergraduate degree is being questioned by a whole mess of folks, including some very well-educated people—people like former US secretary of education William J. Bennett. He wrote a best-selling book, *Is College Worth It?*, that makes a compelling argument that too many people are going to college these days. Compound this with the exorbitant price tag, and many students I talk to question if what they are getting is worth the price they and their parents are paying. One student (a freshman at a private college) that I spoke to complained that on Saturday mornings his school doesn't put any food out for breakfast until 11:00 a.m. because they know all the kids are too hungover to come to the cafeteria before then. "They say they aren't complicit with everyone drinking their asses off, and they totally are, and then they charge $30,000 a semester and pretend it's not happening. It's so bogus."

Another author, Jeffrey Selingo, argues in *College (Un)bound* that the more than $1.4 trillion in debt owed by American students has been frittered away on campuses that focus more on student life than vigorous academics. You may think that a high-tech campus and great parties are the reasons to go to college, but once you check out the price tag, you'll probably agree that earning your money back is at least as important as mastering beer pong. And what if the on-campus experience is postponed for a semester or two? Many undergrads have had to contend with just such a situation during the pandemic. More people than ever have decided to take the leap into gap years and time off instead of ponying up the cash for what might become a virtual experience. Ask yourself: If you can't be guaranteed the social, residential, and sport experiences of being on campus, what is the real value of an institution's online academic instruction? And could you get the same for less somewhere else?

But here's the thing: Education is still the most important investment you can make in yourself for the long term, so I firmly believe you should strive to achieve the *highest level* of education you can responsibly manage. The form in which you get it, however, is up to you. The world is changing. Education is changing, and you can rest assured that the path from high school to college to a job and success is nowhere near as direct as it once was. The cost of a traditional education is different, and so is the value. Unorthodox educations are starting to be treated with more respect, and prestige can come from different sources now.

The questions you need to answer, here and now, are what do *you* want from your education, and how will that education fit into your larger plans for life? How are you going to blaze a trail into your own best future? Yes, more education is expensive, but it really can pay off.

THE DIFFERENCE HIGHER EDUCATION CAN MAKE

Check out this table from the 2017 US Department of Labor Statistics population survey. It shows the extent to which weekly earnings are still tied to diploma level. The data was collected from full-time salaried workers aged twenty-five and older.

Level of Education	Median Weekly Earnings	Unemployment Rate
Less than high school	$520	6.5 percent
High school diploma	$712	4.6 percent
Some college, no degree	$774	4.0 percent
Associate's degree	$836	3.4 percent
Bachelor's degree	$1,173	2.5 percent
Master's degree	$1,401	2.2 percent
Professional degree	$1,836	1.5 percent
Doctoral degree	$1,743	1.5 percent

Source: US Bureau of Labor Statistics, Current Population Survey, 2017

Interestingly, in the five years since the first edition of this book and before the pandemic struck, median weekly earnings had gone up an average of $72 while the unemployment rate went down. The largest drop in unemployment was for those with less than a high school diploma—down 5.9 percent. That all changed in the spring of 2020, when unemployment rose to levels not seen since the Great Depression, approaching 25 percent. Even with stimulus checks and a robust stock market, the future for economic growth remains cloudy. But one thing is for sure: business will need to reevaluate and adapt to a changing reality to survive. And your best bet is

Here are definitions of possible undergraduate certifications and degrees you can complete after high school:

- Certificate or license of training: awarded after completion of one year or less of training in a vocation or trade, often in STEM (science, technology, engineering, and math) fields
- Associate's degree: awarded after completion of two years of study in a course or major at a community college
- Bachelor's degree: awarded after completion of a required number of general and specific credits, most frequently accomplished in three or four years of study in a course or major at a traditional college or university

Where to Get the Degree:

- Short-term courses: programs where you can earn a certificate, diploma, or award in fewer than two years
- Community college: an institution offering associate's or two-year degrees that can be transferred to a four-year program
- Technical/Trade college: short-term, one- to two-year training programs in a variety of subjects
- Four-Year college or university: an institution offering a bachelor's degree in chosen field of study

still on yourself and gaining as much education and training as you can afford.

An associate's degree has better earning potential than a high school degree, and a bachelor's degree can increase your weekly earnings by 60 percent. If you go on to graduate studies or a doctoral degree,

✔ Don't Forget about Debt

When looking at salary statistics, keep in mind that they don't reflect the debt load that many people have to service after they graduate. Yes, your salary is higher, but if you took out loans to get the degree, you have to consider the amount you will need to allot each month to pay off the debt (for an example, see pages 79–80). The goal should be to get a degree that gains you the most advantages and options with the least amount of debt.

the picture gets even better. Many employers won't even interview candidates without a bachelor's or an associate's degree.

But listen up! Even though getting a postsecondary degree is still the best way to make a big difference in your overall chances for a financially solid adult life, *when* you get the degree, *how* you get it, and *where* you get it are nowhere near as important as they once were.

A degree is the certificate that recognizes you've accomplished a certain amount of college coursework credit. The system is designed to help you earn those credits in one place within an established curriculum. However, many students spend years stitching together credits from a few different institutions, take time off, or go study abroad for a year, and ultimately end up with the same degree as a student who spent four consecutive years in one school.

This is where that self-knowledge piece from the first section of this book comes in. If you are a doer with good communication skills,

If you have no idea what you want to do when you get to college, it's probably not worth spending your parents' money or loading yourself with debt until you want to make better use of your time. The same is true if your study skills aren't ready for prime time or if you are sick of school and tired of sitting in a classroom or library. I hate to break it to you: despite what you see in the movies, sitting in a library, going to class, reading textbooks, writing papers, participating in class, giving presentations, and doing experiments—all the stuff of higher learning—are what the whole college business is about. If you feel that the above is a real struggle for you, take a deep breath. You are going to have to think outside the box. You can still go to college; you'll just have to be more careful about where you apply, and you probably would benefit from some extra time and extra help to strengthen your prep skills. Kate Coon, independent educational counselor and veteran college counselor, puts it this way: "Don't be discouraged by iffy grades in high school. Get a GED if you need to. Take a course at a time at your local community college. Build the path one brick at a time."

If more school feels like it might be a good scenario for you after graduation, go back to your pros and cons sheet and put "More School" at the top. As you read through the next chapters, jot down specific pros and cons as they come to mind, and if you have any thoughts on how to turn a con into a pro (for instance, a con might be that you haven't registered yet for the SAT, but you can easily fix that).

sitting in a library studying Chaucer or meditating on the power dynamics of medieval Europe is going to be torture. So why do it? Ultimately, you might be better off getting a trade license from a vocational school that could lead to owning your own business or an associate's degree that could give you a foot in the door in the field of your study. Alternatively, your parents may never have imagined you becoming an arborist, but if you love the field, are trained well by a good program, and can support yourself, why wouldn't you? There is always time to study philosophy or work toward a master's degree in your time off.

In some circles there is still a prejudice against two-year programs, as if the kids who go to community college or trade school are too lazy or dumb to get into "real" college, but that way of thinking is extremely outdated. If there is one thing we've learned as a society, it's that we can't all be scholars and scientists—and many of us don't want to be, anyway. Some of us are builders. Some of us are soldiers. Some of us are artists. Some of us are farmers.

Bank on the fact that the only thing people are going to pay attention to in your adult life is whether or not you can take care of yourself and your family, while you are, hopefully, playing a positive role in the world around you. If you love your work, becoming a paid medical technician, nurse, or welding technician might be better for you in the long run than becoming an English PhD waiting tables. Besides, one does not necessarily cancel the other out. Having a real-world skill can support you financially while you write your novel or study to become an accountant.

Bottom line: You, not your degree, are the measure of your success.

profile

Bill Watterson, cartoonist, creator of *Calvin and Hobbes*

Bill Watterson was born in Washington, DC, in 1958 and moved to Ohio when he was eight. He did reasonably well in school and began to draw cartoons after becoming a fan of the *Peanuts, Krazy Kat*, and *Pogo* comic strips. Watterson went to Kenyon College in 1976, where he spent four years drawing political cartoons for the college campus newspaper, the *Kenyon Collegian*. Upon graduating in 1980, he landed a job as an editorial cartoonist at the *Cincinnati Post*. His bosses didn't like his work and soon fired him, and less than a year later, Watterson was back at home, living with his parents.

Discouraged, he jettisoned the idea of being a political cartoonist and went back to his first love: comics. A long, miserable season of rejection ensued. For the next five years, Watterson tried to keep his sanity by sending strips to newspapers across the nation. Rejection slips and debts piled up, and he put his dreams on hold and went to work as a layout artist for a sleazy tabloid shopper. There, in the dank and windowless basement of a convenience store, submitting to the whims of a difficult boss, Watterson developed that carefree, happy-go-lucky view of life that so permeates all his cartoons.

Looking back, Watterson admitted that this miserable period in his life was an important experience because it cemented in him the belief that the value of his creative work was in his love for it, not in what it earned financially. Meanwhile, at his drawing board, Watterson experimented with many different characters until one day he created a strip called *Calvin and Hobbes*, about an unusual six-year-old boy and his stuffed tiger, Hobbes. Universal Press Syndicate bought the strip in 1985, and soon enough, Watterson became a legend.

Four-Year Colleges and Universities

The brick-and-mortar four-year institution is usually what most people mean when they talk about college. It is the gold standard of postsecondary education in the United States. Here, baccalaureate students graduate after four years of study at a college or university with a bachelor's degree, either in the humanities (called a BA—bachelor of arts) or in the sciences (called a BS—bachelor of science). A university houses several different "colleges" from which students graduate with a bachelor's degree but also has graduate programs that offer advanced degrees, either master's degrees (MFA, MSW, MBA) or doctorate degrees (PhD, MD). A college is dedicated only to four years of baccalaureate education and often has a core curriculum based on the liberal arts (literature, philosophy, mathematics, and social and physical sciences) as opposed to professional and technical curriculum (science, technology, engineering, and manufacturing). The terms can be confusing at first glance because some universities call themselves colleges, such as Dartmouth College, and these terms can have different meanings in other countries. Universities are no less prestigious than colleges and vice versa; they differ only in size, extent of research facilities, and level of degree offered.

Universities can be public or private. Colleges are generally private, but some states have "flagship universities," such as Penn State University or the University of North Carolina at Chapel Hill, that feel more like a college and have a reputation for excellence rivaling that of many private institutions.

Public universities are funded primarily by state funds and proceeds from endowments (gifts or donations). Private colleges and universities rely on private funds, such as endowments, and annual contributions from alumni and donors. Both, of course, with very few exceptions, also rely on tuition payments from students and their families.

These brick-and-mortar schools offer a learning environment that is special and cannot be imitated online: it's where a fluid action-reaction learning experience takes place, in a closed environment, populated by people of all different ethnicities, backgrounds, and cultural values, coexisting, challenging, and learning from one another. Going to college—living with peers on a campus and in close proximity to professors—is like going to a live concert instead of listening to music on your phone. Anything can happen: conversations lead to revelatory moments in and out of class, a challenging teacher becomes your mentor, or people from countries you've never heard of become your friends. For four years, you are held and supported and instructed alongside and by people who are entirely interested in what you are thinking. There is a magic that happens in a college classroom and on a college campus that cannot be reproduced anywhere, and for this reason alone, it is worth considering as an option.

WHAT DO I NEED TO DO?

Okay, you are still reading, so a more traditional, four-year program right after high school still looks like a good scenario. What do you need to know?

Consider this question: What do you want out of a college? Remember what kind of environments encourage you to thrive and take into consideration the following:

- Athletic and other student facilities
- Class size
- Curriculum scope and challenge
- Deferment possibilities
- Dorms
- Faculty
- Financial aid
- Graduation rates
- Level of academic difficulty
- Location
- Off-campus options
- Overall size
- Price
- Public or private
- Social life
- Student housing
- Study abroad opportunities

Then answer this question: What do colleges want from you?

According to a survey of the members of the Independent Educational Consultants Association, colleges look at the following criteria, in order of importance, when considering a candidate:

1. A rigorous high school curriculum that challenges the student.
2. Grades that represent strong effort and an upward trend.
3. Solid scores on standardized tests (SAT, ACT). These should be consistent with high school performance.
4. Passionate involvement in a few activities, demonstrating leadership and initiative. Depth, not breadth, is most important.
5. Letters of recommendation from teachers and guidance counselors that give evidence of integrity, special skills, positive character traits, and an interest in learning.
6. A well-written essay that provides insight into the student's unique personality, values, and goals. The application essay should be thoughtful and highly personal and express a point of view about the topic. It should demonstrate careful and well-constructed writing.
7. Special talents or experiences that will contribute to an interesting and well-rounded student body.
8. Demonstrated leadership in activities. Colleges want people who will arrive prepared and willing to take leadership of student activities and events.
9. Demonstrated intellectual curiosity through reading, school, leisure pursuits, and more.
10. Showing enthusiasm to attend the college, often exhibited by campus visits and, if offered, an interview.

THE OFFER OF COLLEGE

To be at home in all lands and all ages;
To count Nature a familiar acquaintance,
And Art an intimate friend;
To gain a standard for the appreciation of others' work,
And the criticism of your own;
To carry the keys of the world's library in your pocket,
And feel its resources behind you in whatever task you undertake;
To make hosts of friends . . .
Who are to be leaders in all walks of life;
To lose yourself in generous enthusiasms
And cooperate with others for common ends—
This is the offer of the college for the best four years of your life.

—Adapted from the original "Offer of the College"
by William DeWitt Hyde, president of Bowdoin College, 1885–1917

What does this tell you?

First and foremost, colleges like to see you push yourself, so it is better to take more AP, IB, or honors classes and get slightly lower grades than to take easy classes and get As.

It also shows if you have been slacking in the homework department or blowing off due dates for term papers. If this is the case, you'd better get into gear and focus on raising your GPA. Most good schools have an entering freshman class with an average GPA of 3.5,

Colleges, especially those with a liberal arts focus, have always been held in high esteem as a great cultivator of civilization. Because of wage stagnation and automation of the workforce, the marketplace encourages colleges and universities to create more targeted, vocational courses that focus less on the liberal arts and more on preparation for the job market. But what that move gains in skills training, it loses in, well, *soul*. This is a real cost that shouldn't be overlooked when you think about schools. The college years will be a unique time in your life when you get to explore and develop—intellectually, socially, and emotionally. Once you graduate, you will never again have the wealth of possibilities at your fingertips that a good liberal arts college can offer. Additionally, a recent LinkedIn report on workplace trends for 2020 predicts a rebound for liberal arts majors. Ironically, in a future ruled by robots, the "soft" skills of communication, expression, ethics, diplomacy, negotiation, and human resources are expected to grow more and more valuable. So, all you poets, statespeople, and philosophizers, don't despair.

and the best schools want better than that. Don't worry if you haven't gotten serious until now. Colleges also like a comeback story—but the sooner you get things turned around, the better. If you need help, ask your teachers for extra time and guidance or enlist a friend who is good at a subject you stink at to study with you. Use free online academic support services, such as Kahn Academy and HippoCampus, to help you nail difficult concepts in math and science.

COLLEGE ACCEPTANCE TIME LINE

If college is still high on your list, here are the next steps you will need to follow in high school, especially if you are gearing up to apply for a traditional four-year program. The outcome, of course, is your bachelor's degree.

Freshman Year

- Look into honors and advanced classes, and see whether you have the qualifications and prerequisites necessary to take them. Take the hardest level courses you can.
- Try out some different extracurricular activities or sports.

Sophomore Year

- Same as above, but focus on moving into leadership roles in your extracurriculars. Begin to focus your interests. Better to achieve mastery at one thing than to be only okay at a bunch of different things.
- Take the PSAT and assess areas where you can improve.
- Make friends with your teachers and guidance counselor. Get them on your side. Ask for advice on how to maximize your time in school by taking the most challenging classes that you can without flunking.
- Get organized. Turn papers in on time. Show these people that you know how to do the whole "school" thing.
- Make the most of your summer by adding to your skills and experience. Work counts.
- If it applies, get help with weak subjects.

Fall

- Meet with your guidance counselor or independent college adviser. Discuss what you most want in a school and what you don't want. Consider both a two-year and four-year option.
- Work hard on schoolwork.
- Take PSAT in October; assess weaknesses and study.
- Focus on extracurriculars where you are in leadership roles, drop others.
- Have a financial discussion with your parents (for help with this, see chapter 4).

Winter

- Look through college guides and websites, and start making a list of schools you might be interested in.
- Schedule school visits for spring and summer. I would recommend visiting in spring, when there are still students on campus and you can get a better sense of the vibe.
- Take SAT/ACT for the first time.

Spring

- Take SAT/ACT if you didn't in winter.
- Take AP tests and subject tests.
- Visit schools.
- Make a list of favorite teachers who might write your recommendations.

Early Summer/Fall

- Narrow down the list of schools you are going to apply to and request applications.
- Decide if you are going to apply early decision or early action to any schools.
- Download common application.
- Download financial aid and scholarship applications.
- Retake SAT/ACT if needed.
- Fill out all forms and applications.
- Don't slack on schoolwork.
- Get recommendations.

Spring

- Reread this book.
- Construct an alternative plan for a gap year, just in case you want to defer.
- Keep up with schoolwork.

GRADE INEQUALITY

Anyone applying to college in this day and age needs to understand that it is not a level playing field. If two kids walk into the SAT— one who has had six months of prep with an experienced, expensive tutor and one who has not—which one do you think is going to score higher? And the same thing goes for regular classes.

Money can buy tutoring (and lately fraudulent test takers, but that's another matter), which usually translates into a better transcript and puts kids from families with less money at a disadvantage. However, there are ways you can make up the difference without going broke. Free tutoring help is available online, thanks to nonprofit groups like Khan Academy and HippoCampus. Same goes for SAT/ACT prep. Visit collegeboard.org and act.org to take samples of these tests and preview past test questions. There are also a number of skills prep books you can borrow from the library, and some high schools offer free college prep sessions. And if you need help with classwork, don't forget those hardworking teachers! Most of them are willing to work with you after school to help you get into college.

Moreover, this kind of gumption and one-on-one instruction will lead, hopefully, to better teacher recommendations.

STANDARDIZED TESTING

When it comes to standardized testing, most colleges accept the SAT or the ACT, but if you take the ACT, you may also want to take the SAT subject tests. Every college is different, and more and more are going test optional (meaning they don't require the scores) as they come to terms with how arbitrary these scores are to a student's career at college. But thanks to the Common App and the avalanche of applications most colleges receive, they have to have some sort of filter, and at the most competitive schools, these tests are often the easiest way to weed out candidates. Depending on where you are applying, there is a decent chance one of the standardized tests will be necessary. Which one to take is up to you; some kids take both and use the one they score highest on. Plenty of kids take the SAT/ACT two or three times, and occasionally more if they have the money. In 2009 the College Board instituted something called score choice, which allows you to choose which subject scores to send in from various exam sittings, allowing you to cherry-pick your best scores. ACT rolled out their own score choice in September 2020. The more selective schools don't love score choice (which could, in theory, allow a wealthier student to take the tests ten times and still send in the same score as someone who only had to take the test once) and will ask to see all your scores. Some schools will only consider scores from a single test day.

If your scores are still not where you want them to be after the second go-round, consider enrolling in one of the online SAT prep classes. Alternatively, focus on colleges that don't require the test scores and spend more of your energy on getting killer grades. The SAT also offers subject-specific tests in different areas of achievement, and many students take these to supplement the regular required tests. These are hour-long, content-based tests that will help you highlight your genius, even if your regular scores are less than what you hoped for.

WHICH ONE SHOULD I TAKE?

If you plan to take the SAT, you will need to take the PSAT in the fall of your junior year. Most high schools automatically give the PSAT in the sophomore year and again in the junior year, as it can qualify you for a National Merit Scholarship. You can take the real SAT or the ACT in the winter or spring of your junior year and again in the fall of your senior year.

The ACT is an achievement test, or "big picture" test, measuring what a student has learned in school. The SAT is more of an aptitude

The reason to hire an outside college adviser is simple: to help you find the school that is the best fit for you. There's also another reason. According to the US Department of Education, kids in most public high schools receive an average of 38 minutes of personal advising on college admissions, and the ratio of students to counselor is 476:1. This is abysmal for a choice this expensive and important. It's not the school's or the guidance department's fault; it's just a function of low budgets, limited staff, and a whole lot of students. But the alternative of an outside adviser doesn't come cheap (depending on where you live and how much attention you want, the range is anywhere from $3,000–$30,000). You and your parents will have to weigh the benefits versus the costs. To research this option, start by using the search tool of the Independent Educational Consultants Association, iecaonline.com, or talk to someone you know who had a good experience with one.

test, focusing on reasoning and verbal abilities, and was originally designed to be a test you couldn't study for. The ACT has up to five components: English, mathematics, reading, science, and an optional writing test that you take only if required by the college(s) you are applying to. Most traditional universities and colleges do require this section, so it's probably wise to plan on taking it. The SAT has only three components: critical reading, mathematics, and a mandatory writing test. College admissions officers care about how you do on each section of the SAT. On the ACT, they're most concerned with your total score. So if you're weak in one content area but strong in others, you could still end up with a very good ACT score.

RECOMMENDATIONS, EXTRACURRICULAR ACTIVITIES, AND INTERVIEWS

I know it feels like all anyone cares about when it comes to college is grades and scores, but other criteria do matter when you are applying to school. Colleges are less interested these days in well-rounded individual students, but they are very interested in creating a well-rounded class. So if you are a stellar trombonist or hockey player or you can replicate the neural network of a *T. rex* with pipe cleaners or you spent your summer visiting Civil War sites, wear these skills and experiences as badges of honor. Go back to the list of interests in the first section, look at what you circled, and then expound on why. If you've achieved a level of mastery in anything, let them know (even if it's whittling or Ping-Pong). Let the admissions officers revel in your unique skills, interests, and passions, and then get a teacher or two to back you up in their (hopefully sparkling) recommendations. Colleges want to populate their campuses with people who will thrive there. The more you can convince them that one of those people is you, the better your chances of getting in.

One last thing about applying: Schools don't want to know that they are on your B-list, so be eager and enthusiastic in every visit and interview (and be sure to write the name of the school you're actually applying to on your application essay!). Think about why you would be an asset to the campus, and then state the reasons. As you walk around the campus, take notes on your smartphone or a pad. Jot down things you like about that specific school or what went well in the interview (do it then, as you probably won't remember later, even if you think you will). Use that information when you fill out your application to that institution. The more specific you can be, the better. Schools want to know why you like them, and the more truthful and detailed you can be, the more they will like you.

When it's time to start typing, only apply to colleges you would want to go to, even if you are worried about getting into your first, second, or even third choice. Colleges are swamped with applicants these days, so do yourself, them, and your fellow students a favor by not sending the common application to a bunch of safety schools that you don't care about and wouldn't want to enroll in. On the flip side, if you are 100 percent sure that you want to go to a certain school, take the leap and apply early decision (that is, applying early through an early decision program and thereby declaring your intention to attend that given school if admitted). It's a great way to let an admissions officer know that you are serious and loyal, and it might just help you get in.

WHERE SHOULD I APPLY?

There are a mind-blowing number of colleges and universities across the country to choose from, all of which vary in selectivity, academic rigor, graduation rates, and price (among other things). And if you want to go to college, there is a great school out there for you. I swear. If you really want to go, and you can beg, borrow, or work to get there, there is a college out there within your reach. You just have to find it.

Try going back to the start of this chapter and looking at the list of what to consider when thinking about a school. Keep in mind

The ACT has traditionally been more popular in the southern and western parts of the nation, and the SAT in the Northeast, where many of the Ivies are located. If you talk to your parents, they may not even know what the ACT is! Never mind. It's all changing, and even the schools drenched in Ivy respect both tests. The ACT is a good test if you tend to be a literal thinker, and it is a more comfortable

SAT	vs.	ACT
Reasoning test	Type of test	Content-based test
Critical reading: two 30-minute sections Math: two 40-minute sections Writing: one 35-minute essay	Test format	English: one 45-minute section Math: one 60-minute section Reading: one 35-minute section Science: one 35-minute section Writing: one 30-minute essay
Reading, vocabulary, grammar and usage, writing, and math	Content covered	Reading, grammar and usage, math, science, reasoning, and writing (optional)
Questions designed to test reasoning, tricky, difficult to decode	Test style	Direct, questions may be long but straightforward (more like school)

test because it more closely mimics the tests you are already taking in school. The SAT is more abstract and was intended to be a test you can't study for in the normal way (although the extent to which it succeeds can certainly be debated). It challenges you to connect the dots in your thinking. I recommend you take both at least once, see where you land, then go with the one you score highest on.

SAT	vs.	ACT
Math and critical reading will each range from 200–800. The total SAT score ranges from 400–1600. Essay is extra.	Scoring	English, math, reading, and science scores will each range from 1–36. Composite ACT score is the average of your scores on the sections and ranges from 1–36. Essay is extra.
Yes	Score choice?	Yes
Questions increase in difficulty level as you move through a section, except in reading, which moves chronologically.	Difficulty level	Difficulty levels are random.

looking back

"I was a pretty good student and athlete, and I was attending a boarding school that had a little bit of a pipeline to the university where I really wanted to go. At the time, I had no doubt I was going to get in to my first choice. In fact, when I interviewed at the school, the admissions officer basically told me I was a shoo-in. So, you can imagine how upset I was when I got the rejection letter. I couldn't believe it. A classmate of mine had also been rejected, but he came from a family with a lot of money—unlike me. He ended up calling the dean of admissions and asking them to reconsider, which they did. I figured that if it worked for him, it might work for me, so I called up the guy who told me I was going to get in and asked him what happened. He told me he was surprised I didn't get in, but couldn't change it. He did say that if I took the next year to do something really worthwhile and re-apply, he would push my case next time around. So, I took the gamble. I said no to the back-up schools I got into and went to work at a research lab for the year. I reapplied to my first choice the following fall, and got in, and that's where I got my undergraduate degree."

—C. Noble, MD, urologist

all the things we found out about you in the first section, and then start browsing online for colleges that fit your basic criteria. For right now, don't think about the money or how hard it might be to get in; just find a few schools that seem interesting to you. If you have the ability to travel, it's worth visiting a public university, a private university, and a small liberal arts college to get a sense of the essential differences among these categories. (Or you can also take virtual tours online.) Then check out their admission requirements and start to make a list based on your transcript, test scores, and extracurriculars—actually, three lists: reach schools, possible schools, and safety schools. Then let the games begin.

This book cannot even begin to help you sort through all the different schools and their admission requirements, except at a very basic level. Start by working with a college admissions adviser if you can!

Check This: Reach Schools, Possible Schools, and Safety Schools

Reach Schools: Schools that are a reach for you to get into. They are either highly competitive or your profile is on the lower side of what they want. Fate is a fickle mistress, so don't be afraid of having a few reach schools on your list. You never know—you could be just what they are looking for.

Possible Schools: Schools that are within your grasp in one way or another (grades/scores/interests/sports) but still competitive and you are not necessarily a shoo-in. These schools should make up the predominant part of your list.

Safety Schools: Schools you are very confident you can get into. You meet or exceed all their requirements. You should have a few of these on your list and be not only willing but happy to go there if you don't get in anywhere else. (True confession: I went to my safety school after I got dinged early decision by Amherst and wait-listed at Harvard. It turned out to be one of the best things I ever did.)

GETTING STARTED

The following pages provide a very basic rundown of some top colleges and universities to get your wheels turning. This list is in no way complete, but it is a good place to start understanding what traditional college can offer.

All the schools listed in this section have websites you can visit to get real-time information. Please, just start your search with these fabled names. There are so many different colleges, with their own academic thrusts and campus quirks, that it is worth the expense to buy or borrow one of those huge guides, such as the *Princeton Review's Complete Book of Colleges* or the *Fiske Guide to Colleges*, and spend some time with it. (I also highly recommend Loren Pope's *Colleges That Change Lives*.)

LEADING COLLEGES AND UNIVERSITIES

What puts an institution into the top tier of competitive schools? For most people, it's all in the name and all the more so if that name is part of the elite group of East Coast schools that are in the Ivy League (named after their elegant brick buildings draped with ivy). In addition to parental bragging rights and their notoriously competitive admission policies, Ivy League schools and their equivalents across the country all boast expensive, beautiful campuses; top-notch faculty; and a dedicated group of alumni and fundraisers to ensure the best education, student experience, and facilities your tuition dollars can buy. The devil, however, is in the details—what I call the school's "vibe." This has more to do with what it actually feels like to go to school there. Much of a school's vibe comes from its location, ranking, administration, and the ethos

One of the most confusing things about applying to college is the sheer number of schools you could apply to. Midway through junior year, you should come up with a system to help you keep track of schools you like and want to visit or apply to. When Louise Lyall was a rising senior, she did it this way: "If I heard about a college that sounded interesting, I went through a big college guidebook and read about it. Then, if it still looked good to me, I went online and checked out the website and looked it up on Wikipedia. If the school still interested me, I found out what people had to say about it on College Prowler . . . and then I googled pictures of the campus. If, after all that, I still liked the school, I put it on my list." Louise ended up at the University of Wisconsin–Madison.

upon which the school was founded, but the rest comes from that certain something that is harder to put your finger on. It stems from the kind of student the school is attracting and how those students treat one another, handle the workload, and create a (boring or not) social scene. Don't go judging a book by its cover, but here, in a nutshell, is my very subjective take on the vibe of the top categories of several Ivy-esque schools in the country. I haven't personally visited all of them, so I encourage you to visit individual schools yourself before jumping to any conclusions.

These are exclusive institutions and not within reach for everyone, but remember, there are more than 4,000 schools other than the ones listed here. It doesn't have to have ivy clinging to its name to be a great school.

For great insider takes on these schools and many others, check out niche.com and collegeconfidential.com to read real student reviews.

Ivies and Ivy-esque Institutions

These schools are from the nexus of elite academic institutions that most of us think of when we say Ivy League, although technically the Ivy League is all on the East Coast. These institutions are the most competitive, set the bar for excellence in academics and reputation, and are some of the oldest universities in the country—and for this reason, they can look a little worn around the edges. You will be studying a great deal, although rumor has long had it that these top schools are harder to get into than to actually graduate from (Gentleman's C, anyone?). This doesn't mean they are easy by any stretch—just that they are incredibly hard to get into. If you have your eye on one of these golden rings, you will need to ace your classes, chase any advanced placement opportunities you can find, be in the top percentile in your grade, fill your summers with meaningful work, and try to distinguish yourself from the pack in any way possible. But all that hard work should prove to be worth it: a diploma from one of these institutions—regardless of your final transcript—seems to open magical doors in the adult world.

- Brown University
- California Institute of Technology (Caltech)
- Claremont McKenna College
- Columbia University
- Cornell University

- Dartmouth University
- Duke University
- Emory University
- Harvard University
- Harvey Mudd College
- Massachussets Institute of Technology (MIT)
- Miami University (in Ohio)
- Northwestern University
- Princeton University
- Rice University
- Stanford University
- Tulane University
- University of California, Berkeley
- University of California, Los Angeles
- The University of Chicago (UChicago)
- University of Notre Dame
- University of Pennsylvania
- University of Virginia
- Vanderbilt University
- Wake Forest University
- Washington University in St. Louis (WashU)
- Yale University

Small Private Colleges

These schools are small only in terms of relative size (and some sports). When it comes to killer academics, faculty, student experience, and reputation, they are more than equal to their high-powered, larger-sibling universities—except they don't offer graduate degrees. All of the following are private, expensive, and highly competitive, so don't underestimate them. They offer the same (and some would say better and more personal) experience as larger institutions but in a more contained setting, with an intimate class size and living situation (read: dating scene can get a little claustrophobic). In some cases, these smaller schools will have an exchange agreement with surrounding schools that allows you to expand your horizons by taking classes off campus.

- Amherst College
- Barnard College
- Bates College
- Bowdoin College
- Bryn Mawr College
- Carleton College
- Coe College
- Colby College
- Colorado College
- Connecticut College
- Denison University
- Grinnell College
- Hamilton College
- Hastings College
- Kenyon College
- Macalester College
- Middlebury College
- Mount Holyoke College
- Northwestern College
- Oberlin College
- Pomona College
- Radcliffe College
- Ripon College
- Smith College
- Swarthmore College
- Vassar College
- Wellesley College
- Wheaton College
- Whitman College
- Williams College

Top Public Colleges and Universities

In addition to many already listed above, the following schools are public institutions with the selectivity, challenging curriculum, history, and alumni success to rival any private school. What they lack in private funds, they more than make up for in tradition, school spirit, and relative financial accessibility. If you live in a state that can lay claim to one of these schools, all power to you: you may be in reach of a top-notch education for one-third of what the rest of the country has to pay. State universities are large and include a healthy graduate-degree student population, which means many introductory sessions may be taught by graduate students (as opposed to lectures, which are almost always given by tenured professors). The state universities all have satellites in other towns within their home state—some campuses may not have the status of their more famous flagship campuses but will still get some of the glow—and are easier to get into, and once you are in, you can more easily transfer to the campus of your choice.

- Arizona State University
- Clemson University
- Florida State University
- Ohio State University
- Purdue University
- University of California
- University of Georgia
- University of Massachusetts
- University of Michigan
- University of Minnesota
- University of New Hampshire
- University of North Carolina
- University of Texas
- University of Utah
- University of Vermont
- University of Virginia
- University of Wisconsin

Alternative Colleges and Universities

These schools are part of the changing face of education and have a lot to offer the less buttoned-up student. They are distinguished in that they offer a different kind of education, and often lifestyle, than the more buttoned-up schools. Most are respected four-year institutions with all the college amenities, although many also offer low-residency degrees and online classes. Curricula at these schools is student-driven but as challenging as or more so than other schools—and their tuition is on par with their traditional counterparts too. The main difference is in the nature of that curriculum—which usually has a more holistic or artistic bent—and the faculty that provides it, which supports the values that the school espouses. These kinds of schools pay more attention to the individual and creative pursuits of their applicants and care less about test scores and grades. The emphasis is on being fully present and engaged with your learning and the world around you, not just clocking in credits toward a degree. Once you get in, you'll have more freedom to design your own coursework and major in collaboration with your professors.

For more information on these schools, plus an expanded listing of alternative programs by state, visit educationrevolution.org.

- Antioch College
- Bard College
- Bennington College
- Berea College
- California Institute of Integral Studies
- College of the Atlantic
- Cornell College
- Deep Springs College
- Earlham College
- The Evergreen State College
- Franconia College
- Goddard College
- Hampshire College
- Hofstra University
- Maharishi University of Management

- Marlboro College
- Naropa University
- New College of Florida
- The New School
- Pitzer College
- Prescott College
- Reed College
- Sarah Lawrence College
- St. John's College
- Thomas Edison State University
- Warren Wilson College

And Don't Forget Art School

The kids who go to art school aren't necessarily undecided; they tend to know that they are miserable unless they are making something or doing something artistic (I'm talking to you, creative doers). Art school is college, however, and though you will focus on studying the fine arts under faculty who are professional artists, you will also (usually) take courses in English and history and science and math, just like anywhere else. So, if you like the idea of going to a school where your primary focus will be cultivating your artistic expression, then art school should be right up your alley. It is also a good training ground for those of you who like tagging, graphic arts, packaging design, computer and graphic design, architecture, theater, and making models. Art school has its own grad network, which means that an important part of the experience is that you will build friendships and contacts with like-minded people who can help you make your way in the world on a very tough career path. Art school is not any cheaper than a traditional college. In fact, it's often more expensive because of all the supplies. If the price puts it out of your reach, look hard at the art departments in more traditional institutions. Some liberal arts colleges have phenomenal art departments. Another alternative is to get your BA at a traditional school and then get your master's in fine arts (MFA) when it will be easier to work and pay for it.

Here's a short list of top art schools to start your search:

- California College of the Arts
- California Institute of the Arts
- Carnegie Mellon University

- Cleveland Institute of Art
- Cranbrook Academy of Art
- Maine College of Art
- Massachusetts College of Art and Design (MassArt)
- Parsons School of Design
- Pratt Institute
- Purchase College
- Rhode Island School of Design
- San Francisco Art Institute
- School of the Art Institute of Chicago
- School of Visual Arts
- UNCSA School of Drama

Last but Not Least: STEM Schools

For those LEGO-builders, puzzle solvers, and bridge-builders, there is a whole group of high-ranking schools that lead the way in STEM (science, technology, engineering, and math) degrees.

- California Institute of Technology (CalTech)
- Carnegie Mellon University
- Colorado School of Mines
- Georgia Institute of Technology
- Maine Maritime Academy
- Massachusetts Institute of Technology (MIT)
- Missouri University of Science and Technology
- Rice University
- Rochester Institute of Technology
- Texas A&M—College Station
- Texas Tech University

- University of Illinois–Urbana-Champaign
- University of Southern California
- Virginia Tech
- Worchester Polytechnic Institute

Two-Year Colleges

Two-year colleges are local community colleges that award an associate's degree, a nursing degree, or some kind of apprenticeship license or professional certificate after one or two years of study. They are a great way to further your education without going to a traditional four-year program. Some community colleges offer vocational, or trade, instruction in addition to academics.

Community colleges, as a rule, are designed to educate students of all ages and abilities, and offer flexible schedules that can be arranged to suit work and family life outside of school. Often called providers of "further education" (that is, of continuing education for people who might otherwise consider their school days to have passed) as well as of higher education more generally, community colleges teach a wide array of enrichment courses and also have standard college curricula. A lot of undergraduate students these days attend community college for the first two years and then transfer to a traditional four-year program as a way to lower cost. This may be the new face of higher education as life gets more expensive and complicated.

Enrolling in community colleges is easy. Most schools have an open admission policy, which means that any student with a high school diploma or equivalent is welcome. In that case, your grades in high school don't even matter. Nor do your SAT or ACT scores. Once you sign up, community colleges insist that you take a standard aptitude test for placement purposes. They often offer remedial classes for students who need to catch up in certain trouble areas, like math or science or reading. These schools are thus excellent choices for anyone wanting to improve English language skills or gain experience in a certain field. Some of the hot courses in community colleges are those geared toward STEM occupations, advanced manufacturing and robotics, health-care professions like nursing, pharmacology, and radiologic technology, and high-paying trade professions such as electrical work and plumbing.

One real-life bonus of gaining an associate's degree at a good community college is that you can go straight into the workforce with little to no debt, and you have a very good chance of quickly paying off whatever debt you have accrued. Community colleges and trade schools are a much cheaper option than four-year programs because you pay for your education by the credit hour, plus they add the extra bonus of flexible scheduling so you can hold down a job while you study and, possibly, live at home.

THE HIDDEN COSTS OF TRANSFERRING

Transferring from one college to another is common nowadays, and it's a good thing. The cost is so high that you should move if you are unhappy or if the campus life and curriculum is not serving you. Be prepared to lose up to a semester in credits, though, especially if the school you are leaving has a core curriculum or proprietary classes for freshmen. This is the dirty little secret of transferring. It's almost as if colleges and universities have a backdoor agreement to not accept the equivalent of a semester of credits when a transfer student is accepted. This shouldn't be a big deal if you can take on an extra course load, but in most cases, it will mean you have to make up credits (and pay for them) over the summer or online at your new school if you want to graduate on time.

Thomas J. Snyder, former president of Ivy Tech Community College in Indiana, wrote that "a community college education can make you more employable and enable you to earn significantly more than the average liberal arts major with a bachelor's degree." This is because the job market of the twenty-first century is looking for the kind of manufacturing and high-tech skills that community colleges specialize in. He also states that at Ivy Tech graduates more than double their earning power by attending community college, which means they make about a 16 percent return on their investment in their education. He also reports that 31 percent of graduates with an associate's degree earn more than their peers with a bachelor's degree. So, if the ability to earn money and have maximum flexibility are high on your list, a two-year program at your community college could be for you. And if you don't have the competitive edge (or the funds) to get into the four-year college you want, check out your local CC. It is a great starting point.

I say this knowing that in some circles there is still some snobby blowback about attending a CC. One sixteen-year-old boy I spoke with put it this way: "If I can't get into a real college, there's no way I'm going to a CC. It's like admitting to everyone that I'm a dumbass." He is not alone in feeling this way. For many kids, going to a community college may be perceived by some friends and family as a kind of failure. But this is outdated thinking. At the risk of sounding like a broken record, I'll repeat: in the adult universe, it only matters what you know how to do, not where you learned it.

In these uncertain times, flexibility and competency are traits workers of the future are going to need. Automation is quickly making mincemeat out of what were once considered to be "steady"

✓ A Class Sampler

Not all two-year credits are transferable. It depends largely on what you study and what school you want to transfer into. For more information on how to transfer from a two-year college to a four-year program and how to get financial help doing it, visit CollegeFish.org and bigfuture.collegeboard.org.

Some of the classes offered by the local community college make me want to sign up and go myself. Here's a smattering pulled from my local community college's 2018–2019 course catalog:

- Acting: Body and Voice
- Advanced Pastry and Baking
- Arabic
- Disease Pathology/Diagnostic Digital Electronics
- History of Science
- Introduction to Geographic Information Systems
- Jewelry and Metalsmithing
- Marine Design
- Medical Ethics and Law
- Microeconomics
- Neonatology and Pediatrics
- Police Procedures
- Public Safety, Survival, and Wellness
- Sport Psychology
- Tree Fruit Production
- The Twentieth-Century Novel
- Ultrasound Physics
- World History since 1500

jobs, while fewer folks are training in certified professions— but IMHO, the future is going to rely on those who are both intellectual and capable—with the chops to make the bacon and fry it up in a pan. Community colleges are a terrific place to explore this merger. Many famous and accomplished people started out at community colleges, including actors Morgan Freeman and Tom

profile

Tina Fey, writer, comedian, actor, entertainer

Fey was born in the suburbs of Philadelphia in 1970. A self-described happy-go-lucky "supergeek" in high school, she writes in her memoir *Bossy Pants* about how dorky she was growing up. She describes herself as awkward and shy as a kid but also "kinda funny." By middle school, she liked wisecracking and getting laughs. Fey wrote an independent study school report on comedy in eighth grade and watched TV comedies like *Laverne & Shirley* and *Happy Days*. Her older brother reenacted skits from *Saturday Night Live* for her, since she wasn't allowed to stay up and watch.

Fey had dreams of becoming a performer, but in high school she began to discover that she liked writing and was "probably a little better at it." She went to the University of Virginia right after high school and studied playwriting and acting. After graduating with a BA in drama, she went to Chicago and joined Second City, which could be considered a kind of comedy trade school. For her, it was the best of both worlds: writing her own material and Second City comedians performing it. In 1997 Fey earned a spot at *Saturday Night Live* as a writer and performer, and went on to become head writer. Fey has won nine Emmy awards, three Golden Globe Awards, five Screen Actors Guild Awards, and numerous Writers Guild Awards. She's written a best-selling book and two hit movies.

Hanks, filmmaker George Lucas, journalist Jim Lehrer, United Farm Workers CCO and founder Dolores Huerta, space pilot Eileen Collins, and scientist and human genome decoder Craig Venter.

Trade Schools and For-Profit Schools

Do you have a gift for cutting hair or a knack for knitting? Do you like to learn through hands-on work? Do your friends tell you that you would be a great chef, jewelry maker, stylist, or mechanic? Maybe you are interested in a high-value career in IT, health care, engineering, or automotive technology. Or maybe you just want to know how to do something useful and do it well. If any of this sounds like you, going to a trade school to become certified in a targeted skill should be high on your list of postgrad options.

Trade schools are career-oriented and are open to everyone—not just high school or college students. They offer short-term training and certification in a wide array of fields, including animal care, computers and technology, design and graphic arts, cosmetology and aesthetics, cuisine, health care and physical therapy, travel and hospitality, legal services and criminal justice, business, and medical tech. Skilled trades, such as plumbing, automotive and electrical repair, HVAC, aviation, and professional transport, also require special kinds of certification. Many of these certifications are also offered through community colleges. In today's economy, getting a license or certificate from a reputable trade school can be good for your wallet, even if the skill you are getting licensed in is not ultimately part of your dream plan. Not all of us belong in a traditional college environment, but that doesn't mean we can't still learn a lot of different valuable skills after high school graduation. By obtaining a trade school certificate, you prove to potential employers that you have the aptitude and ability to do a very specific kind of work that not just anyone can do. Depending on the trade you learn, there is a high likelihood of a job waiting for you when you get your license. And depending on the requirements, you could be ready for work in as little as two weeks.

On the con side, private trade schools can often be, well, problematic at best. They offer zero academic instruction, unlike a community college. Plus, they are not usually cheap. The entry of big business into the trade school sphere has made it a cash cow for for-profit education investors (more dirt on private, for-profit schools in a moment). The major chains may make grand claims about their educational standards and starting salary rates, but it's not a good idea to rely on those assurances. And while it's true you may graduate trade school with a job, you need to get real about what kind of job you will get. This is where talking to former students from the school is helpful. Additionally, use your phone and google the school you are thinking about. Read the comments before you make any decisions. In my area, the first comment on the nearest private trade school says, "This isn't a school, it's a flat-out business trying to take your money." The next one talked about how much debt going there got them in.

If, despite all my warnings, a private trade school still seems like the best bet (do the pros and cons sheet!), getting certified can take anywhere from two weeks to two months to a year or two, depending on the skill you are training for. Skilled and hazardous trades often require an additional period of apprenticeship and on-the-job experience before you can obtain a journeyman's license. Do your due diligence. If the best, fastest way to get a license is through a private trade school, make sure it is accredited by the Accrediting Commission of Career Schools and Colleges. You can do this easily by visiting their website at accsc.org.

Some trade schools operate brick-and-mortar campuses, and others are distance-based and offer what used to be called correspondence classes. Be wary of any program that advertises pie-in-the-sky salary projections and job offerings, however. You'll have to take a long, hard look at the tuition requirements and compare the cost with that of similar classes at your local community college. If a program is going to lure you with such bold claims, you should force it to make a convincing case. If the school has a campus, visit it and talk to currently enrolled students. Ask to speak with alums of a trade school you are interested in. If the school can't provide contact information, it usually means they can't find someone who had a positive experience, and it's definitely time to move on.

Different states require different certifications to be considered licensed (that is, legally sanctioned to practice the given trade or craft). If you want to work with people—for example, as an aesthetician, massage therapist, yoga teacher, or hairstylist—you will need to research your state code, as well as any on-the-job or apprenticeship requirements. If you are interested in a skilled trade or craft, you must complete the experience hours (usually a minimum of four years or eight thousand hours) and be able to perform a specific trade without supervision. You must pass an exam in that trade to qualify for a journeyman's license.

ARTISTIC TRADE SCHOOLS

Trade schools aren't just for vocational students. If you want professional training in the performing arts, film, music, or creative writing, there are a lot of paid programs out there that you can enroll in with little to no experience. Here's a short list of some good ones, and if you live in or near an urban center, you can find plenty more just by searching—but be careful of the cost! Some can cost upward of $30K a year for a degree or certification.

Creative Writing

- 826 Valencia (826valencia.org)
- GrubStreet (grubstreet.org)
- The New School (newschool.edu)

- Groundlings (groundlings.com)
- Lee Strasberg Theatre and Film Institute (strasberg.edu)
- Second City (secondcity.com)
- Studio A.C.T. at American Conservatory Theater (act–sf.org)

Film/Documentary

- Film Connection (filmconnection.com)
- Los Angeles Film School (lafilm.edu)
- Maine Media Workshops (mainemedia.edu)

FINDING THE RIGHT PROGRAM

Before you enroll in a trade school, be sure it's *actually* a school and can issue a real certification or associate's or bachelor's degree. Get a full understanding of what the school provides: how much instruction and what kind, the supplies needed, and the degree you'll receive upon completion. Research the instructors, including their job experience and their qualifications. The Federal Trade Commission also suggests that you gauge the success of any for-profit trade school program by looking at the following criteria and asking the following questions:

Completion rate. How many students drop out of the program? Why?

Job placement. How many graduates get jobs in their chosen field?

Salary. What can you expect? What are graduates actually paid?

Cost. What is the total cost? Do they charge by the course? Semester? Program? What if you drop out or add courses? Are there other expenses, such as books or supplies?

Debt. Of recent graduates, how many have debt? How much? How easily are they paying it off?

As in all things, personal recommendations are the best source of information. If there are professionals in your town who are doing what you would like to do, ask them about their experience. Where did they train? Or go online and research businesses that hire in the field. Call and talk to the human resources person or the manager. Ask what the business is looking for in an employee and which trade schools do the best job.

If you come away with anything from this book, I hope it is an understanding that dreams are built one brick at a time, and you need to be able to take care of yourself as you build them. If this means you work by day as a licensed aesthetician at a spa while you write poetry at night, at least your license will provide you with the income to get the tools you need to write the poetry (including food, shelter, and notepads). We live in a complicated world, and your approach to it should be equally multifaceted. Having a variety of proven skills will only serve you. Just be careful about where you learn those skills and how much they ask you to pay for the instruction.

FOR-PROFIT SCHOOLS

Proprietary, for-profit universities, such as the University of Phoenix and DeVry University, are operated by businesses and corporations and offer the ability to get a degree or trade certification either in person or online. However, let me be crystal clear: They are in the business of making money. To date, they enroll about 12 percent of all postsecondary school students and gear their curricula to lower income, adult, and working students. These colleges, like trade schools, design their curricula with specific job training in mind, and some of the more respected ones got their start as "college completion" schools, where students finished off their educations after already completing two years of study but failing to get the desired degree.

A lot has changed since the 1990s, when these schools were founded. They have turned almost exclusively to Wall Street for financing. This means they are run as businesses and must please stockholders and investors first—not students. And they are notorious for crashing and burning. Since 2018, 95.5 percent of all colleges that closed have been for-profit schools. Overnight they can declare bankruptcy and leave you high and dry, holding on to your worthless credits and no refund on your tuition. This is a big deal if you've taken out loans to go because you will have to pay those, regardless. Moreover, 95 percent of the credits from for-profit schools won't be transferable to a public or community college.

For-profit schools also have the highest ratio of student debt versus tuition, the lowest return on investment (meaning it's harder to find a good job with one of their degrees), and a higher dropout rate (it's way easier to blow off class when your teacher is in your computer, not a classroom). Virtually all (96 percent) of the students at for-profit schools borrow money, whereas only 13 percent of students at community colleges, 48 percent at four-year public schools, and 57 percent at four-year private nonprofit colleges borrow to pay tuition.

Many of these for-profit schools target first-generation immigrant and low-income students who may or may not be aware of the options offered by state and community colleges. Plus, even as they rake in earned income, these schools chow down on students' federal aid. This would be okay if a student could be ensured a good education, but the quality is really spotty at these places, and chances are you won't finish—eight out of ten students drop out. Whether you learn anything or finish doesn't matter to the suits; either way, you are contracted to pay the full price.

In general, this book is intended to provide you with the information you need to come up with your own plan and work things out in your own way. But this one case is an exception, and I want to make a basic fact plain: I do not recommend for-profit schools unless you are really, really, really stuck. Even then, check out all your other options first, including state and community colleges, before signing a contract. If you do sign up, read the small print carefully and buyer beware. If you are unsure of whether or not a school is for-profit, google it. Its status will appear on its Wikipedia page. If it is a for-profit school, understand its priorities (making as much profit as possible) and know you are not at the top of the list. Shop accordingly, and do not go into a ton of debt to buy this degree unless you are very confident you can make back your investment.

Distance Learning and Studying Abroad

Here's a welcome relief in the education conversation. Distance learning: the twenty-first-century version of the correspondence course. By now, you will have had your own experience with distance—or remote—learning, so you know better than me how it suits you. It isn't perfect, not by a long shot, but distance learning is still a good choice if you are unable to attend a brick-and-mortar campus or vocational school, or as a supplement to other courses. Distance education courses can be presented as live, interactive audio- or videoconferencing; streaming webcasts; or computer-based systems accessed over the internet. Nowadays, most brick-and-mortar schools also offer online components to their curriculum in what's called a "hybrid" experience.

First, the upside: Distance learning is a quick, great way to learn at less cost. All you need is access to a computer and the internet, and you can take as many classes as you can handle without ever having to leave your house. Everything you need, including instruction, syllabi, reading material, and tests, is provided electronically. If you need to keep a job, take care of kids or parents, or can't afford to attend school in person, distance learning might be the answer. You are also free to work toward your degree or certification at your own pace. The bummer side? You have to make yourself log on and do the work with no one but your own conscience to prompt you. It's an isolated, lonelier way to learn and requires a lot of motivation and self-discipline. Yes, you will be able to chat with fellow students online, but that is not the same as sitting in a classroom and walking around campus with them. The experience is also not a great choice if you like to work with your hands. Moreover, there is, at this point in time, no good way to gauge the quality of an online course except by judging the institution offering the program. You also need to get accepted to an accredited program and then opt in for the online component. Do not pay for an online course run by a for-profit business unless the company you work for compensates you directly for the tuition.

We learned from the COVID-19 lockdown experiment of 2020 that remote learning has a real down side, and that 2D classrooms are not the solution we thought they might be. Students and professors reported missing the energy and spontaneity of live classrooms, and the actual experience of learning online can be exhausting and dispiriting. The term "Zoomed Out" entered our

profile

Stephen Hawking, physicist

Stephen Hawking was born on January 8, 1942, in the United Kingdom, three hundred years to the day after the death of Galileo. He is now widely considered to be the most influential physicist since Einstein, rocking the world of physics in 1974 with his groundbreaking research on black holes.

You would think that this kind of brain was a shoo-in for academia, right? Not so fast. In his early years, Hawking struggled with school. He was very bright and liked math, but he was not the brightest in his class (though his nickname was Einstein, so his classmates must have seen something in him). At one point in high school, he did so poorly that he ranked third from the bottom of his class. Hawking preferred to do things outside of school; his family kept bees and made fireworks in the basement. He liked to disassemble clocks and radios, build models, and play board games. He invented new games of his own with his friends. At age sixteen, Hawking and some of his friends made their own computer out of recycled parts and used it to solve math problems. At age seventeen, he went to University College. The school did not have a math major, so, lucky for us, he agreed to study physics.

His continuous exploration into the underpinnings of the universe has changed the way scientists view time and space, cosmology, quantum mechanics, and the origins of the universe. Hawking died in 2018 from a progressive nerve disease called amyotrophic lateral sclerosis (more commonly known as ALS, or Lou Gehrig's disease), which he was diagnosed with at the age of twenty-one.

lexicon, and given their druthers, most students would choose to actually get up and *go* to school (imagine that!). Yet online learning does do the trick in a pinch. Your experience will largely depend on your access to technology and the ability of the professor to translate and embody the curriculum for the digital sphere (read: not every professor can do it well). It is—for sure—easier on the wallet. In reaction to the pandemic shutdowns, most colleges and universities have scrambled to create fully operational online platforms for their students. I think it is safe to say that the online college universe will only get better and sleeker as things evolve. Some institutions already offer full-fledged degrees online. Some of the largest are Penn State, Purdue (which bought the for-profit college Kaplan University for one dollar and transformed it into an accredited online component called Purdue University Global), UMassOnline (the University of Massachusetts's online education consortium with UMass Amherst, Boston, Dartmouth, Lowell, and UMass Medical School), and Arizona State University. These online degrees are adjunct with the school, which means you have to apply to the actual institution and be accepted in order to qualify to go digital.

STUDYING ABROAD

If you are fluent in a particular language or have a parent from another country or even have an obsession with a specific culture or region in the world, applying to a foreign university may be an option worth considering, since many schools in other countries charge far less tuition, and some may even be free. About 3 percent of US college students are enrolled in full-degree programs outside the country, according to a 2015–2016 report by the Institute of International Education's Open Doors project. This does not reflect the huge rise in students studying overseas on short-term study abroad programs (for a semester or over the summer). I'm talking about applying and going to an international university as a full-time student.

You can solve the language problem by going to school in English-speaking countries (Canada, England, Scotland, Ireland, Australia, New Zealand, and so on). Or, as I mentioned earlier, you could opt for a semester or a year or two and transfer your earned credits. Most competitive US colleges and universities have gotten hip to the idea that students want to study abroad, at least for some of their college life, and will boast of their international programs and alliances to get you to stay in their lane. Usually this means an easier time transferring credits and less headache paying tuition and fees but less choice.

If you want to get your undergraduate degree overseas, know that most foreign universities and accredited study abroad programs (that will help you enroll in a foreign university) do have bachelor degree programs, as well as postgraduate degrees.

Aside from the obvious benefits (language immersion, exposure to a different culture, becoming a global citizen with friends from around the world), studying abroad can be a less expensive option than attending a US school. Many South American and European countries regard higher education as a right rather than a privilege, and their tuitions and fees reflect this belief. However, the housing and facilities can leave a lot to be desired for American students used to more luxury, and the instruction style is very different from what you might be used to. In general, you'll get a lot less hand-holding.

If you apply to a foreign university on your own steam, you should expect to be treated just like any other native student subject to all the attendant rules, government-mandated curriculum, and regulations of that institution and culture. If you go through a study abroad program like Center for Study Abroad (centerforstudyabroad.com) or GlobalLinks Learning Abroad (globalinksabroad.org), they will help you search and apply for the right university and degree program and serve as an advocate for you when you are overseas. Transitions Abroad (TransitionsAbroad.com) is a good online clearinghouse that will link you into various study abroad programs by destination. Another good place to do research is your guidance counselor's office.

The most important criteria to consider when thinking about studying abroad are:

- Destination
- Cost of living
- Language aptitude
- Subject of study or desired degree
- Accreditation of school and transferable credit or diploma
- Price
- Housing availability
- Travel costs
- Visa restrictions

Federal financial aid and scholarships are available for students wanting to study abroad. The National Association of Foreign Student Advisers (nafsa.org) has a great website that will help you figure out how much cash you will need (based on your desired destination, institution, length of study, and so on) and where to find help with funding. If you are nervous about making a commitment for three to four years, you could always try studying abroad for a semester or a summer session while you are still in high school.

Foreign universities are beginning to accept the common application and US standardized test scores, but they do things differently. Be prepared to apply and to test ahead of time into a specific subject or college within the university system. For example, if you want to study history, you will apply to the academic department or college

✓ **Check This: Classes on the Cheap**

Nothing is free, but these schools come close.

These European schools offer an excellent education for very low tuition (the same as their own population pays), but the cost of living can be high. In some cases, you will need to know the native language.

- University of Bergen
- University of Oslo
- University of Iceland
- Free University of Berlin
- University of Vienna
- University of Warsaw
- University of Freiburg
- Anglo-American University

that instructs history. Don't be afraid to do your research into the requirements, and then take the test and see what happens. Studying overseas could be a great option, as it combines both college and broad life experience that can only enhance your skills as an adult. For more information on traveling and working abroad, see chapter 20.

Many foreign universities offer a bachelor's degree within three years (in contrast to four here) because the curriculum is more specialized. Let's say you want to go to Oxford University in England. There are no major or minor subjects, only a single course of study (one subject) or joint honors courses (two subjects). Subjects are taught in lectures and tutorial sessions consisting of a tutor and you (and possibly one other student). The onus of work is on you.

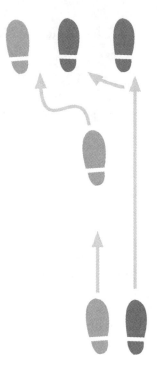

When you choose the paradigm of service, it turns everything you do from a job into a gift.

—*Oprah Winfrey, Stanford Class of 2008 commencement address*

part three:
service

What You Need to Know

One alternative open to you directly after high school—or even now while you are still in high school—is service, otherwise known as volunteering. At the heart of this path is a desire to offer your skills and energy in support of an ideal that is much larger than yourself. That ideal might be working for a political campaign or grassroots organization, educating people, protecting the environment, or serving your country, but the willingness to do service comes from a drive to do something meaningful and big. Often this drive is personal, or it can be passed down to you from your family, your religious exploration, or a mentor who has inspired you. We live in a world that has a massive need for smart, energetic young people who care about making a difference. Because the willingness to do service comes from an internal orientation, it is also a way to work at things you like to do, which is different from a regular job or internship, where you will spend a lot of time doing things that other people tell you to do.

Volunteering allows you more personal choice around how you spend your days, and if you go back to part one and look at your temperament and preferences, you will probably know right away whether that is important to you. And if you don't know whether or not it is important, service can be a great way to experiment with different educational and career opportunities. It's amazing how much you can do if payment is not a priority.

You may think this advice is conflicting in regard to military or civil service, where mission and orders rule over personal choice. But think about it: if you love to work with animals or bungee jump or take apart the microwave in your spare time, those interests can be cultivated—for free—as part of your training and service in these arenas. Also, as you advance in both military and civil service, you will eventually get paid, which can often be the case when you start out as a volunteer.

Volunteering is a magic door opener, and you may find yourself doing some pretty high-level stuff if you position yourself in the right place and work hard. Connections are essential to placement and advancement, no matter what field you wind up working in. Thus, in addition to work experience, you could gain a foot in the door at a point where normally you'd still be stuck outside or stockpile a handful of killer references. It's a tough job market out there, and every little bit helps.

Entering into service or volunteering in your community is also a fast track out of the doldrums. If you're bored, uninspired, or at a loss of what to do with your time and the prospect of going straight into more school feels like the last thing you want to do, helping others can be the fastest way to help yourself. Doing a stint at a nonprofit or learning the ropes as an unpaid volunteer in a field that seems sort of cool is an easy means of expanding your perspective and your skills in ways you can't anticipate now. It can also provide you the opportunity to find out what really matters to you and possibly to travel and learn in distant places.

Many people who are interested in service already have an altruistic bent. Whether they know it or not, they tend to value relationships, experience, and charity as their own kinds of compensation. Like I said, this bent may come naturally or may be passed down as part of your family's value system. And it may come simply from feeling fulfilled after volunteering—even if it's just helping a neighbor unload her groceries or cuddling dogs at a local animal shelter. No amount of money can buy the feeling of being the object of sincere appreciation and gratitude, and when you mix in the ideal of helping the common good—well, that is money (in a karmic sense). But not everyone who ends up doing service knows ahead of time that they'll like it—nor do they have to be selfless. In fact, at this point in your life, doing service can originate from a place of real self-interest.

One of the hardest things for young people to acquire is experience. It's a catch-22, because you need to get a job to gain experience, but most jobs require people to have some previous experience.

A big question to ask yourself when looking at service-oriented options is why. Why are you interested in this particular form of service? What's in it for you? Just because you're in service to others doesn't mean your intentions need to be altogether selfless. Plenty of people join military service because of the job opportunities and benefits. Travel, life experience, and good karma are just a few other good reasons to volunteer for a nonprofit organization or at a school, either here or abroad. And there are plenty of other reasons. Volunteering can be a great litmus test for different fields you're interested in, without having to take a full-time job. You can feel free to try various vocations. Commit to a regular short stint of service somewhere, just a few hours a week, and see if it's a good fit. If it isn't, be honest about it, move on, and try something else. Schools, nonprofits, and other organizations are always looking for volunteers. There's never a shortage of opportunities. A quick search on volunteermatch.org or idealist.org will yield hundreds of options. Go ahead and take a look!

Going into service to gain some real, hands-on practice in the world is just as legitimate a reason as going in with high ideals. Let's say two people volunteer to build houses for Habitat for Humanity. One is doing it because he wants to help lift families out of poverty. Another is doing it because she wants to gain practical skills and meet people, and helping a family is a nice bonus.

Either way, the results are the same: a family gains a new home and the mission of the organization is served. The inner motivation of the volunteer is thus, in a way, almost beside the point. So don't count service out, even if you don't consider yourself the type. Dollars to doughnuts, service offers you the most varied, personally rewarding, and open-ended path into the future. What's more, you don't need a lot of skills to go into service. While it may seem counterintuitive to volunteer your time (instead of getting paid for it), the training and connections while doing it can be a lasting stepping-stone by boosting your résumé when you apply for further education or paid work.

A 2013 report put out by the Corporation for National and Community Service found that volunteers have a 27 percent higher chance of finding employment over fellow candidates who did not volunteer. If you eventually want to go to college, taking time off to volunteer at an organization can be a real eye-opener that will help you focus on what you want to accomplish at school when you go back to your studies.

But this alternative is not for everyone, especially if you're not the kind of person who does especially well with long-term planning or commitments. You need sincere passion and commitment to the organization or cause you are providing service for, for as long as you agree to work, because once you sign on, it may be hard to turn back—particularly if you sign a contract with the military or a civil service program. Also, many of these organizations are understaffed and overstretched, so they will quickly come to rely on you—which is, generally speaking, a good thing! Start by talking to other people who have chosen a life of service, such as veterans, chaplains, social workers, civil servants, activists, and Red Cross and other nonprofit volunteers. If you simply want to try volunteering, start now and start small, maybe even in your own neighborhood. Begin with something you love to do. If you like to read, check out your local library and see if they need volunteers to go into schools and read to children. If you like to play soccer, ask your local YMCA or Boys and Girls Club of America if you can help coach. Or see if your school has a club that focuses on community service.

Different kinds of service are needed everywhere. To get you started, I've provided links throughout this section to the best online search sites for you to browse.

Military Service

Of all the branches of service you could go into, the military offers more benefits and training than any other while asking for a greater sacrifice. There are plenty of reasons to join. Maybe there's a history of military service in your family, and you want to continue that legacy. Maybe the traditions, physical challenges, and lifestyle of a soldier call to you. Or maybe you've heard how a stint in the military can help pay for college and provide different kinds of benefits and job training. Or you might want to see the world and do something significant. Or maybe you don't have any other options because of your financial situation. All are good and valid reasons. The military offers the most benefits and job security of any major employer around, as well as a sense of well-deserved pride for serving and protecting one's country.

But here's what you need to know before you sign anything: in exchange for taking you in and training you—both mentally and physically—to become a warrior on land, on sea, or in the skies, the US armed forces require that you be ready to fight for your country and put yourself in harm's way if called to do so. The minimum term of enlistment is eight years, with optional retirement after twenty years of service and mandatory retirement after thirty. Once you sign the contract that enlists you in the armed forces, the military owns you for the term of your contract. Chances are extremely good you will be deployed and you might see combat action or at the very least be part of the support for combat troops in theaters of battle around the world. After all, the US has been at war now for 18 years.

In this service, you may be hurt, killed, maimed, or psychologically traumatized while on active duty. You cannot quit or back out of the terms of your contract once it is signed, or you could face dishonorable discharge, desertion charges, and possibly imprisonment. I say this right off because I want you to make the decision to volunteer for military service seriously, with a lot of forethought and discussion with the people who love you. You may think it's easier to keep your plans to enlist a secret, but don't. Those people you want to deceive are the ones who will suffer the most should anything happen to you when you are deployed. They should have a chance to voice their concerns.

Does the exposure to danger mean you shouldn't volunteer for the military? No, not necessarily. Life is a dangerous business, and the upside of joining the military can be a game-changer given the right circumstances. But go in with your eyes wide open. Do not sign any contract (for any course of action, for that matter) without reading it, understanding it, and discussing it with your parents and loved ones.

Understand that your personal values are not relevant to the agenda of the armed forces, and by signing up you tacitly agree to surrender those values to the wisdom and endeavors of our nation's chief military officers. Also keep in mind that military battles are real and deadly, not a video game with resets. Know what you are getting into before you go, because your life is on the line.

BRANCHES OF THE MILITARY

Military service in the United States is divided into five branches: Army, Marine Corps, Navy, Air Force, and Coast Guard. Each service has its own history and traditions, and finding the right one can be tricky—it all depends on what you want to gain and what you can contribute while enlisted. This is part of the reason the military relies so heavily on recruiters. They are trained to answer all of your questions and steer you into the right branch of service. But before you start that process, think back to the lists you made in the first chapter. Do you love the idea of travel? If so, maybe the Navy or the Coast Guard would be for you—you would spend much of your enlisted time aboard one of the hundreds of ships in domestic waters or abroad. Does the tradition and lifestyle of a soldier particularly fit you? Do you love a challenge? Then the Marines could be your calling. Either way, each branch offers hundreds of jobs and positions to choose from.

High-tech to low-tech, abroad or domestic, there's bound to be an opportunity that matches your particular skills and interests. To determine this, every potential service member has to have a high school diploma or equivalent. Then they must take the Armed Services Vocational Aptitude Battery (ASVAB). This standardized test is split up into eight separate tests:

- General Science
- Arithmetic
- Word Knowledge
- Paragraph Comprehension
- Mathematics Knowledge
- Electronics Information
- Auto and Shop Information
- Mechanical Comprehension

Your scores and answers on each test will help military recruiters determine what kinds of jobs you'll be best suited for. Score higher on the math and science side? You could be on the electronics, engineering, or nuclear propulsion track! Maybe the test determined that you're more inclined toward media relations or construction or mechanical work or linguistics—or any number of other fields. The ASVAB will help figure where and how you'll fit within the military. But first, you've got to choose which branch.

BENEFITS OF JOINING THE MILITARY

I've already made the risks and perils of joining the military pretty clear, so let's take a look now at the possible benefits of military service—many of which are quite substantial.

In exchange for completing your tour of duty, the military offers an astounding array of educational and career-training opportunities that will translate well into civilian life, including human and recreational services, health care, media and public affairs, STEM services, business and clerical administration, law enforcement and firefighting services, food prep and delivery, vehicle and machinery mechanics, construction and repair trades, electrical trades, machine operating and technological precision work, and transportation and cargo handling skills.

The military offers money for education, health and dental care, and at least thirty paid vacation days per year. There are also other perks, such as free room and board (or a food and housing stipend), a clothing allowance, and free use of all the on-site recreational services. Depending on your length of service, your health and insurance benefits could be available to you for life, as well as a pension and retirement plan. As a veteran you will be able to receive free health care at any VA hospital in the nation.

During your service, your base pay scale will go up or down depending on your promotions and attending duties. Certain special commissions and active combat service receive additional cash bonuses. If you graduate from Officer Candidate School, you will receive an officer commission, with commensurate rank, pay, and additional benefits.

WHAT ARE THE EDUCATION BENEFITS?
The biggest source of military education benefits comes from the G.I. Bill. After you've given a minimum of thirty-six months of honorable, active-duty service, the G.I. Bill will pay for all tuition and fees for the next fifteen years (up to the cost of in-state tuition—so watch out for that). And in addition to covering tuition

and fees, you can receive a living allowance to cover housing costs and a stipend to cover books and supplies. The new, revamped G.I. Bill also has provisions allowing service members with at least ten years of active duty to transfer their benefit to a spouse or dependent family member.

If these aspects of the G.I. Bill don't cover all of your education expenses, the Yellow Ribbon Program can help supplement it. This program, only available through partner universities and colleges, functions by having set amounts—each school determines its contribution—that are matched by the Department of Veterans Affairs. A particular school may limit the number of students who can receive a Yellow Ribbon match. Furthermore, restrictions may govern whether the program applies to specific degrees or programs of study. You can find a list of participating schools at gibill.va.gov. Remember, though, the only way to know for sure is to check with the school you're interested in—so give it a call and ask!

SERVICE ACADEMIES

If you know beyond a reasonable doubt that you want a career in the military, and you are a top student and in good physical shape, you might be able to get a stellar college education and become an officer in the military branch of your choice simultaneously by applying to one of the nation's elite military service academies. As respected (or perhaps more so) as any of the Ivy League or Ivy-esque universities, these lauded schools are notoriously difficult to get into (averaging an acceptance rate of 7 to 9 percent). In addition to overall academic and athletic excellence and a strict sense of honor and discipline, these academies require a nomination from a US Congressperson to be considered for acceptance. You may not be married, pregnant, or responsible for any children when you apply. If you are one of the chosen few, the perks are considerable: you will not have to pay for tuition, books, medical and dental expenses, or food and living accommodations while you are there. Instead, you repay the country with your service for a period of years after graduation. Unlike other schools, you must begin the admission process your junior year by interviewing and getting a nomination from your congressional representative.

- United States Air Force Academy at Colorado Springs, CO
- United States Coast Guard Academy at New London, CT
- United States Merchant Marine Academy at Kings Point, NY
- United States Military Academy at West Point, NY
- United States Naval Academy at Annapolis, MD

SENIOR MILITARY COLLEGES

The following senior military colleges offer students the option to pursue military training while they're enrolled. Unlike the service academies, there is no service requirement after graduation unless you receive a Reserve Officers' Training Corps (ROTC) scholarship.

- The Citadel
- Norwich University
- Texas A&M
- University of North Georgia

- Virginia Military Institute (VMI)
- Virginia Tech
- Virginia Women's Institute for Leadership at Mary Baldwin College

ROTC

ROTC scholarships are awarded in the Army, Navy, and Air Force branches of the military. They are available for durations of four, three, or two years and are specifically geared toward both current high school and college students. With an ROTC scholarship, you attend college like everyone else, only the military pays your way. You will also take specialized classes that will assist in your service. (For instance, if you are awarded an Air Force ROTC, you will have to take some classes in aeronautics.) There are over 1,100 college campuses that have ROTC units on campus, as well as several junior and senior military colleges. All of them allow you to graduate with a degree in a chosen college major and to receive a commission as an officer in your chosen field of service.

✓ **An Eye on Benefits**

Many benefits kick in only if you complete your tour of duty and fulfill the obligations set forth in your military contract. So read the fine print! Medical problems and emergencies that might force you to withdraw from active duty can happen. Make sure you know what the requirements are before you enroll in a school.

Each branch of the armed forces has its own particular course requirements and incentives for students on an ROTC scholarship, but general eligibility requirements for a four-year ROTC scholarship are below. You must

- be a US citizen
- be between the ages of 17 and 26
- be between 60 and 80 inches tall (men), 58 and 80 inches tall (women)
- be at a reasonable weight or willing to lose weight if you are overweight (to check requirements go to operationmilitarykids .org to see acceptable weight ranges for your gender, height, and age)
- have a high school GPA of at least 2.50
- have a high school diploma or equivalent
- score a minimum of 920 on the SAT (math/verbal) or 19 on the ACT (excluding the required writing test scores)
- Score a 31 or above (based on branch requirements) on the Armed Services Aptitude Battery test
- meet physical standards

In exchange, you commit to serve full time for four years in the Army, Navy, or Air Force—whichever branch gave you your scholarship. The only exception to this is for the Marine Corps. Their scholarships are distributed through the Navy.

WHICH BRANCH IS RIGHT FOR ME?

Army

The oldest of the US military branches, the Army currently consists of more than 500,000 soldiers, our country's boots on the ground. It has three ways to serve: active Army, Army Reserve/National Guard, and ROTC. The Army Reserves and National Guard offer the opportunity to become a citizen-soldier, ready to serve when needed. All recruits undergo Basic Combat Training (BCT)—a

Get Your Bearings

Each branch of the armed forces has an individual website where you can learn more about their specific benefits, incentives, scholarships, support services, and career opportunities and how they differ:

- TodaysMilitary.com
- GoArmy.com
- GoArmy.com/rotc
- Navy.com
- Marines.com
- Airforce.com
- GoCoastGuard.com

The Army website lets you read blogs from soldiers serving overseas, as well as connect with parents of soldiers. These sites will also help you find colleges with an ROTC unit. If you like what you read, you can ask for more information to be sent to you or visit your local recruitment office and talk with a recruiter. It is the recruiter's job to tell you the truth about joining the military. Of course, they are going to sugarcoat some of the more difficult aspects of military life, but you should know that each of the services have regulations that make it a crime for recruiters to lie, cheat, or accept candidates that are not eligible. It is their job to get you to join if you are eligible, but you are fully capable of doing your own research too.

rigorous nine-week period meant to turn you into a soldier. Once you complete this, you undergo Advanced Individual Training, which gives you hands-on training on in-field instruction to teach you how to do your own specific job. Ongoing training is available as you move your way through the ranks, and includes Leadership Training, Unit Training, and Specialized Schools. There are over 150 jobs available through the Army, most of which are easily transferable into civilian life.

There is a difference between being on active duty in the Army and an Army Reservist. You may enlist as a Reservist, but you can be called up to active duty at any time if there is a national need. But don't be naive about this—soldiers are desperately needed right now, and you will probably be called up. On the other hand, if the Army sounds too mild for you, you might consider joining the Army Rangers, an elite special operations squad that is very intense.

Navy

The Navy is unique in that it fights our battles on land, in the air, and most importantly—since 70 percent of Earth's surface is covered in water—on the seas. It was formed during the Revolutionary War to protect colonial ships from British attacks. Nowadays, as a part of the Navy, you could find yourself aboard one of the hundreds of deployable ships and submarines traveling to nearly a hundred international ports. The Navy's mission is manifold but includes maritime domination. According to their website, two of the top priorities are to serve as a guardian for America's freedom and life as we know it, and to facilitate the safe travel of people and goods to meet the expanding demands of globalization.

If traveling is your thing, the Navy could be a good option for you, although maybe not if you're prone to seasickness. At any given time, up to 40 percent of the Navy is shipped out overseas, so be prepared to be away from home. Because the duties and missions are so varied, the Navy also serves as a diverse professional training ground. You could find yourself studying nuclear engineering or becoming an attorney with the Judge Advocate General's Corps (JAG) or a physician or chaplain. The Navy is also home to the Naval Special Warfare community, which tackles the most demanding missions. These members include the elite branch of special operations forces: the Navy SEALs.

Marines

The Marines are a special breed and are considered the point of the military's spear. They are first and foremost considered riflemen because their training emphasizes good marksmanship. The Marine Corps develop a fierce loyalty within their ranks, honed during the twelve weeks of intense Marine Corps Recruit Training, where recruits become lean, mean, fighting machines.

The Marines are typically the first troops on the ground in a conflict, and recruiters will tell you that "the values of Honor, Courage, and Commitment inform everything a Marine does." If you are interested in the Marine Corps, you will have to meet all the regular armed forces eligibility requirements (which I'll spell out in a moment) and score much higher than average on the

Initial Strength Test, which consists of pull-ups for men and flexed arm hangs for women, crunches, and a timed run. Every year you are in active service, you will need to pass this test, as well as the standard physical fitness test and a combat fitness test. Becoming a Marine is a tremendous test of will and self-discipline, qualities that will go on to serve you well in just about any career you have as a civilian.

Air Force

The Air Force was originally under the command of the Army, but since the middle of the twentieth century, it has been its own entity.

As you can tell by the name, the Air Force fights our battles in the skies. It has bases throughout the United States and the rest of the world, so there's ample opportunity for travel as you work as a mechanic, pilot, flight crew member, air traffic controller, or any of the other essential positions. Only 4 percent of the Air Force are pilots; 96 percent serve and train in more than 140 other careers, including health care, science, law, and engineering. It is considered the most flexible of the branches, with a high crossover into civilian jobs.

As a member of the Air Force, you will graduate from the Community College of the Air Force (CCAF), which offers sixty-seven degree programs in more than eighty fields of study. You are automatically enrolled in CCAF when you enlist and earn college credit as you go through the Air Force training.

Coast Guard

While it may be the smallest division of the military (with only 40,000 full-time service members), the Coast Guard serves a perpetual "peacetime mission" protecting our coastline and waterways and serving as police in American waters. Coast Guard stations are dotted all along our shores, and if you like to live at or near the sea, this could be a great option for you with much less risk of life and limb than if you enlist in other branches of the service. Many of the positions in the Coast Guard transfer well to civilian life, and over 8,000 people currently serve part time (only one weekend a month and two weeks every year). As a member of the Reserve Coast Guard, you generally serve at a station within 100 miles of your residence, and many reservists are students or hold down other jobs. But be aware that as a reservist, you can be called up to active duty at any time should there be a need. In addition to guarding, the Coast Guard offers career paths in environmental or marine science, law enforcement, and engineering.

PHYSICAL FITNESS REQUIREMENTS

If you are serious about joining the military, you must be at least seventeen (with parents' permission). You will undergo a physical examination to assess any health condition or concern that might make you unfit to serve. To serve you must be

- free of contagious diseases that would likely endanger the health of other personnel
- free of medical conditions or physical defects that would require excessive time lost from duty for necessary treatment or

hospitalization or that would likely result in separation from the military for medical unfitness
- medically capable of satisfactorily completing required training
- medically adaptable to the military environment without the necessity of geographical area limitations
- medically capable of performing duties without aggravation of existing physical defects or medical conditions

If you pass this basic examination, as well as your ASVAB aptitude tests, you will be enrolled and enter into basic training, otherwise known as boot camp. You've probably seen a few movies that give a sense (if somewhat exaggerated) of what boot camp is like: screaming drill sergeants, endless push-ups and sit-ups, running for miles, combat exercises, and coursework. According to the United States Armed Services website, TodaysMilitary.com, basic training "prepares recruits for all elements of service: physical, mental, and emotional." It gives service members the basic tools necessary to perform the roles that will be asked of them for the duration of their tour. Each of the services has its own training program, tailoring the curriculum to the specialized nature of its role in the military.

No matter which branch of the service a recruit chooses, basic training is an intense experience. However, 91 percent of recruits complete their first six months of service. The purpose of this training isn't to "break" recruits. Rather, the combination of physical training, field exercises, and classroom time makes individuals strong and capable. It's a tough process but a rewarding one that many service members value for life.

That being said, basic training is certainly no picnic. It can include twenty-hour days with very little sleep, serious physical challenges, and a lot of mental training to prepare you for the stress of combat. Once you are through basic training, you will be required to take the Army Physical Fitness Test (APFT) twice a year, which measures repetitions of sit-ups and push-ups, and has a timed two-mile run.

PREPARING FOR LIFE IN THE MILITARY

In order to enlist, you must meet the academic, physical, and other requirements noted previously. You must be a US citizen or be a legal permanent resident physically living in the United States with a green card.

If you like to smoke marijuana every now and then (as surveys suggest many teenagers do), get ready to stop. In fact, all recreational drugs are off-limits. The military "uses random, no-notice urinalysis," and—if you're found positive—you may very well go to jail (as well as being dishonorably discharged).

Tier 1 candidates have a high school diploma; Tier 2 have a GED or have been homeschooled. You should have a clean criminal history and no record of drug use. You should have a clean mental bill of health, with no history of psychosis or insanity, and be judged to be of good moral character. Plus, your participation must prove consistent with the interests of national security.

To do well in boot camp, you should get into shape beforehand: regular cardio workouts, weight training, push-ups, and sit-ups are good to start. It's also not a bad idea to become your own drill

looking back

"I never had a big plan to join the military. I didn't do very well in high school so college was not an option for me at the time, and I really didn't want to do more school. I came from a small town, and I didn't have much money, and there were no real job opportunities there. I could have gone to work at the local grocery, but that was about it. A friend of mine had gone into the Navy as an air traffic controller, and that seemed pretty good. I didn't have a better plan, so I thought I'd enlist and get a slot as an air traffic controller. They offered me Army Infantry. I got a lot of money for signing up and a chance to travel. Plus, after I did my tour, I could use the G.I. Bill for a college education. The Army gave me a plan; it gave me something to do that seemed meaningful and exciting, and it gave me a decent salary and benefits. Granted, it was peacetime, but still, given the same choices, I would do it again. The only time I thought I'd made a mistake was when the bus pulled up to boot camp and the drill sergeants got on the bus, yelling. There is practically no veteran I know who did not have a serious moment of doubt at that time. You just have to remember, they can't kill you in boot camp. And once I completed those weeks of training, I never felt stronger or more confident. I served four years of active duty and four years of reserves. My Infantry training hasn't translated as well as some to my occupation now, but the skills I learned in the Army have served me: self-discipline; the ability to see a job through; the ability to endure intense stress and intense periods of boredom—plus, I'm a good shot. When I got out, I was able to go to college and, eventually, to buy my own home, all thanks to my service benefits. My only advice to anyone thinking of going in is, if you have the grades, it's preferable to go in as an officer through ROTC or the academies. You get better pay, benefits, and training. The military is not for everyone, but for me, it was the right choice."

—T. Vose, information technology specialist

sergeant and practice sticking to a strict schedule of rising and bedtime. Before you go, delegate any responsibilities to another family member or friend. You are not going to be able to do anything but train for a while.

Once you complete your terms of service, your training in the military will help position you for many careers in a variety of different fields, from lawyer to doctor to law enforcement, politics, or business. The discipline you will learn in the military will serve you remarkably well, as will the extraordinary experiences you have while you are enlisted, and you will receive this training for free.

A BIG DECISION

As I said in the beginning, joining the armed forces is a very serious decision. Once you sign up and are shipped out to boot camp, you have officially left civilian life. You can't withdraw from the military as you can a school. Nor can you quit as you would a dissatisfying job. If you're late for your post or disobey a superior's direction, you aren't just going to get fired—you can be court-martialed and placed under confinement. Granted, it's unlikely this would happen for a minor offense, but the rules are completely different from those of a civilian job, and you've got to keep that under consideration.

While on active duty, you will always be under someone's command. (Even generals are under the command of the commander in chief!) A superior officer will provide your orders, and you will have to abide by them. If they say clean the toilet with your toothbrush, you clean the toilet with your toothbrush. These

✓ Women and Transgender Personnel in the Military

Women now compose up to 16 percent of the military and are allowed to serve on the front lines and in combat roles. However, the military does still have the right to discriminate by gender. In April 2019 the Trump administration banned all transgender personnel from serving or enlisting in the armed forces in their transitioned gender. As of this writing, that ban is still in place.

Women may now serve in formerly closed armed combat roles, but it is still an active controversy. Like any environment where men and women live together, abuses can happen. This is even more likely when you add the high stress of battle, close living quarters, uneven ratio of men to women, and a rigid rank-and-file system that makes it hard for victims to report their abusers. And let's not forget that the military is notoriously macho. The #MeToo movement has helped to make public many cases of sexual harassment, rape, and discrimination of women in the military. If you are female, this is an issue to talk about with your parents and recruiter. Things are getting better for women in the military, but sexual discrimination and abuse does exist, and you need to be prepared.

orders will be your law. If that doesn't agree with you, you should certainly see that as a major warning sign. If you have trouble with authority, the military is probably not the place to iron out that particular wrinkle.

Finally, there is one vital thing that has been in the background of this conversation about the military. It's always there, but among all the other aspects of the military, it can be strangely overlooked. As a member of any of the armed forces, you may face the possibility, and indeed the duty, of performing a willful and ordered act of violence toward another human being. If this is abhorrent to you (as it is to many), seriously consider how it will impact you to train for and execute this kind of order.

After you take in all of this, I suggest you talk to others. Have a family member in the service? Ask them about the experience. A recruiter will try to woo you with the best aspects of enlisting while glossing over the less desirable aspects. Talk to your parents

profile

Colin Powell, military official, diplomat

Colin Powell was born in 1937 in Harlem, New York. His parents were Jamaican immigrants who moved to the South Bronx to raise their family. Powell went to New York City public schools and graduated from Morris High School, totally undecided about what to do next. He enrolled at City College and earned a bachelor's degree in geology. He also enlisted in the ROTC at the City University of New York and soon found the direction that would shape his life. He quickly rose through the ranks to become commander of his unit. He graduated from college in 1958 and served two tours in Vietnam, and during the second he was injured in a helicopter accident. He also served in South Korea. Powell has received eleven military decorations in his lifetime. Later, he went on to get an MBA from George Washington University and to serve under every US president from Jimmy Carter to George W. Bush. In 2001 he was appointed secretary of state under President George W. Bush, which was the highest political office ever achieved by an African American until the election of President Barack Obama.

about joining. Discuss the matter with your friends. Ask the hard questions: What exactly are you expecting to gain? Are you looking for a job or a calling? Do you have the capacity and moral code that allows for ordered violence? How long of a commitment would you be willing to make? How many times have you said "yes, sir" in your life—and are you willing to let that number increase exponentially?

If, after reading this, you still want to look into the military, make it your plan A and list out the pros and cons; the next step is to do more research online, talk to your family, other past or present members of the military and, finally, a recruiter. But don't sign anything yet! There are still more choices, as the rest of this book will show. The more options you consider, the more you can rest assured in whatever decision you ultimately make.

Civil Service

There are many ways to make a big difference without joining the military, and one of the most stable areas is to work as a civil servant. Many people have lifetime careers as civil servants, whether they become police officers, firefighters, politicians, postal workers, transportation authorities, park rangers, FEMA (Federal Emergency Management Agency) workers, or a number of other careers available in national government. Civil service means working in the public sector for a government agency, often in some form of public administration or law enforcement. But there is also a different kind of civil service you can experiment with right after high school, before you decide whether or not you want to make a career out of serving others. The federal government has created a number of civilian-based service organizations to gather volunteers interested in serving their country internally by helping to foster education; eradicate illiteracy, homelessness, and poverty; and steward our physical environment.

One such group was the Civilian Conservation Corps (CCC), established during the Great Depression by President Franklin D. Roosevelt. In 1933 he called on the citizenry of our country (who were largely unemployed and suffering at that time) and put them to work to revitalize the economy by creating the CCC. It was one of the most popular programs of the New Deal. Four million youth signed up and helped to plant nearly three billion trees and developed more than 800 national parks before it was shut down by Congress in 1942. Since then, the government has looked for people to join different branches of a modern kind of civilian corps and strengthen our nation's infrastructure. You can find specifics about all of them at nationalservice.gov, but here is a basic breakdown:

AMERICORPS

Sometimes referred to as the "domestic Peace Corps," AmeriCorps is the umbrella term for three separate but related programs that specialize in doing just that—spreading peace domestically. This is the main civil service organization in the United States, and it's worth getting to know the separate arms and how they function. There's Volunteers in Service to America (VISTA), which places members in some of our poorest urban and rural areas around the country for a year in the hopes of bringing individuals and communities out of poverty. Next up is AmeriCorps State and National, which functions similarly (and also offers part-time opportunities). Finally, there is the National Civilian Community

Corps (NCCC), where team members work on assignments around the nation. But let's drill down a little deeper.

Volunteers in Service to America (VISTA) operates under the auspices of a specific goal—to help eradicate poverty in the United States. It was started by President Lyndon Johnson in 1965 and was incorporated into AmeriCorps in 1993 by President Bill Clinton. You can search for VISTA sites all around the country via the AmeriCorps website or by doing a search on a nonprofit and volunteer listing site such as idealist.org for AmeriCorps/VISTA. As a VISTA member, you will serve for a year on a specific project at a nonprofit organization or public agency in exchange for a modest living allowance and health benefits. VISTA members develop programs to meet a need, write grants, and recruit volunteers. They often work in support positions and help build financial, administrative, and organizational capacity within the program they are serving. Some positions require a college degree, while others do not. It depends on the organization or agency you will be serving. There are opportunities in education, health care, community building, arts programming, literacy efforts, and economic development. After you serve, you could be a candidate to receive a Segal AmeriCorps Education Award or post-service stipend to help with college.

With VISTA, you will serve the mission of poverty eradication, and in return, you will receive several (modest) benefits. First is a living allowance. The amount is based on the location of your service site but is locked in at 105 percent of the local poverty level. This meager pay is somewhat offset by other benefits. If you have to travel or move to your site, you may be eligible for a transportation stipend. Health care is provided, and childcare is available as well. One of the kickers is the choice of receiving either a Segal AmeriCorps Education Award ($6,195 in 2020) or a $1,500 stipend at the end of your year-long term. Also, since your income is so near the poverty level, you should be eligible for some form of SNAP, or the food stamp program, through the local office of the Department of Health and Human Services.

NCCC

The National Civilian Community Corps is open to eighteen- to twenty-four-year-olds interested in performing national and community service. As a part of NCCC, you'll work as a member of an eight- to twelve-person team and are required to complete a minimum of 1,700 hours of service, including 80 independent service hours. Over 1,000 corps members and team leaders are chosen each year to serve at one of four regional campuses, located in California, Colorado, Mississipi, and Iowa. Each campus serves a multistate region. You will be trained in CPR, first aid, public safety, and other skills before beginning your first service project. NCCC is open to all US citizens, nationals, and lawful permanent resident aliens.

As an NCCC member, you may provide disaster relief as a part of the FEMA corps, or you could work in national parks and in wilderness conservation areas building and repairing hiking trails. NCCC members receive a $4,000 living stipend for a ten-month term and free housing, meals, uniforms, and medical benefits. After your ten months of service, you're eligible for a Segal AmeriCorps

looking back

"I moved back home to North Conway, New Hampshire, after graduating college in 2010. I worked odd jobs for a year or so, saving money while I tried to figure out what I was going to do with the rest of my life. I felt unfulfilled in my work but paralyzed by job searches and didn't know where to begin to start a career. A college friend told me about a program through AmeriCorps where you got to live in tents and work outside. I learned the program mission was to empower young adults through hands-on conservation service and education. I applied for a member position, got it, and loved it.

"There were seven of us (five members and two crew leaders) that worked and lived together in Baxter State Park in Maine in a little cabin for three months. I learned a lot in those three months. I became better at working with a team with different personalities and developed a much better work ethic. My self-confidence grew with the new skills I had gained, and I got in really good shape from hiking so often. Sure, the bugs weren't always fun to work around, you don't get paid a whole lot, and sometimes the weather wasn't cooperative, but we learned to be flexible and have fun with it, because we were all in it together, and we all wanted to be there. That job ended in November, but I wasn't ready for it to be over. During the winter I applied as a crew leader for the Montana Conservation Corps, and I got it. This position is one of the most fulfilling jobs I have ever had."

—*S. Wright, Montana Conservation Corps*

Education Award. There are different NCCC options you can research via the AmeriCorps website (serviceyear.org) or the Corps Network, which functions as a clearinghouse for each state's corps efforts.

As an AmeriCorps State and National member, you will work directly at community service project sites throughout the country. This program is very similar to VISTA, but as a member, you often will be engaged in more direct service with community members or your host site, such as tutoring or mentoring. AmeriCorps State and National programs are open to US citizens, nationals, and lawful permanent resident aliens ages seventeen and up. Members serve full or part time over a period no longer than twelve months. Full-time members are given a living allowance; health care; childcare, if they qualify; and become eligible for the Segal AmeriCorps Education Award upon successful completion of service.

IS IT FOR ME?

Becoming an AmeriCorps member is an option that has few downsides for those who are motivated to serve. However, you need to be able to keep an open and tolerant mindset that is focused on helping others—not judging them. Many of the people you will help may not speak English as their first language, they may be immigrants from very violent and poverty-stricken countries that have their own culture and values, and they may resent the fact that they need your help. Charity can certainly be helpful, but it is rarely a compliment. As part of the NCCC, you may encounter tragedy and disaster, and a whole lot of human misery. In any of these positions, you will have to work hard for relatively little pay and face some very adult realities about the world we live in.

This is not an option for the fainthearted, or for people who don't want to get their hands dirty. It is, in its own way, as life-changing

profile

Elizabeth Warren, teacher, activist, senator

Elizabeth Warren was born in Oklahoma City in 1949. Her dad made a living doing odd jobs, including being a maintenance man at an apartment complex, until he suffered a heart attack. The heart attack resulted in massive medical bills that destabilized the family's finances. Warren began helping her struggling parents at age thirteen by working as a server in her aunt's restaurant. In high school, she was an excellent student and a state debate champion. She graduated at sixteen with a full scholarship to George Washington University. She spent two years there before dropping out to marry her high school sweetheart and moving to Texas.

Warren graduated in 1970 from the University of Houston. She earned a BS in speech pathology and audiology, becoming the first person in her family to graduate college. She and her husband moved to New Jersey and had two children. As a young wife and mother, Warren worked in the public schools helping kids with disabilities until her oldest child turned two. She then attended law school at Rutgers University. After graduating in 1976, she practiced law out of her living room. By 1978 she had divorced her husband and started to research the reasons why so many Americans ended up in bankruptcy court. She taught at the universities of Texas, Michigan, and Pennsylvania, and then became a professor at Harvard Law School in 1995. That same year, Warren was tapped to be the chief adviser to the National Bankruptcy Review Commission. In 2008 she was appointed chair of the Congressional Oversight Panel monitoring the bank bailout effort, formally known as TARP (Troubled Asset Relief Program). Four years later, she was elected to the US Senate, and in 2020 she ran for president of the United States with a platform true to her background as an outspoken champion for the rights of the middle class and families.

and challenging as military service (though it lacks the stress of potential combat and life-threatening situations). And many of the benefits are similarly modest (often more so). You will engage in hands-on professional career training working for an organization or agency. You will get to know parts of yourself you didn't realize existed, and you will receive the honor and gratitude that comes with national service. You will experience situations and problems that might permanently alter your perspective. You may also earn money toward furthering your education if you complete your term of service. That term is relatively short, which allows you plenty of time to pursue other goals. And if you want to go to college eventually, a stint in AmeriCorps is an impressive thing to have on your résumé.

If you are interested in checking out civil service opportunities, go to your plan and put *civil service* on the first line. Your next step is to go online and do more research at each of the individual sites so you can look at the pros and cons of one program over another. Once you decide on a program, call the contact number on the website and ask them to send you the most up-to-date information on opportunities, benefits, and housing. Then discuss it with your parents.

Foreign Service

The Peace Corps is probably the best-known foreign service organization. If you want to join the Peace Corps directly out of high school, you're going to need some pretty special credentials—otherwise, you might be out of luck until you've beefed up your skills, résumé, or education. The average age of a Peace Corps volunteer is twenty-eight, but there are many other programs suited to people aged eighteen and older. Volunteering overseas can be achieved in many ways. I include the most accessible, nationally known options, but don't forget to check your local church, temple, or other religious organization. Many of these groups partner with mission-based service trips that have room for teens who want to do meaningful work. You will have to square with their mission first, but this is a good way to go if your funds are limited. If they aren't, look at the fee-based programs mentioned in this section. The fees charged are used to offset housing, food, and support costs. The prices can be eye-popping, but when you compare the tuition for college or other training programs against what you stand to gain in travel and experience (and good karma), the cost seems reasonable for the benefits.

To get the lowdown on what you are going to need while traveling abroad, see chapter 10, but also know that if you are going with an organized group, you'll receive a lot of assistance with these details, as well as recommendations for any insurance or medical necessities before you go. Most of these groups monitor the news and will not intentionally place you in a dangerous region. However, some groups do provide aid to countries that have the potential for violence, so it's good to stay current with international events. The State Department posts an up-to-date list of travel warnings for countries where long-term problems and changing climate make a country unstable or dangerous to travel in (state.gov). As I said, if you volunteer through a credible program, your safety and travel should not be a problem. Your comfort levels might be a little challenged, but that also depends on where you go and what your expectations are.

If you choose to volunteer overseas with a group, you'll go with a bunch of like-minded people—and there is nothing like working together for a common cause to create lifelong bonds of friendship. If you go alone, you will probably be housed with a family or have some other kind of homestay option that will give you a window into the lives of people who live in the region. You may even become like one of the family if you stay long enough. You will also be doing meaningful work that will have an immediate impact on the people you go to serve. Your language fluency will improve, and you will learn a great many new skills, not the least of which is how to travel and make a home for yourself in another country. Depending on your budget and length of stay, you may be able to travel home on vacation or for holidays, and your family will certainly be able to visit you.

Because there are so many options available now to volunteer abroad (especially if you can pay), I recommend going back to your core value worksheet and start by identifying a personal volunteer "mission" statement that aligns with those values (for instance, if you are outdoorsy and energetic, you might want to volunteer helping to build infrastructure somewhere). When you look for a program, also keep in mind the goals of the organization and consider its impact. The best organizations are working with communities to help them succeed long term. Often the best programs are smaller and more specific (like building a school or helping in a medical clinic). Keep in mind these qualities when looking for a reputable program:

1. The program is run and has impact on a local level (local resources, local administrators, sustainable community projects).
2. The program maintains a record of results (long-term benefits, years in operation, etc.) and references.
3. The program provides good communication and preparation to help you ready yourself for the work and travel to the destination.

WHAT ARE SOME GOOD ORGANIZATIONS?

Below are a few organizations with which to start your foreign service search.

Volunteers for Peace

Volunteers for Peace (VFP) has been sending people ages eighteen and older on individual and group service adventures across the globe since 1948. VFP offers over three thousand projects in more than a hundred countries through a network of partner organizations. The goal is to find you a project that meets your needs and helps fulfill a need in a local community. According to the website (VFP.org), there are three types of projects:

Work camps. Volunteer with people from four or more countries for a two-to three-week service project, building cultural understanding and meeting a local need.

Individual service adventures. Create a personalized two-week to one-year international service project.

Group projects. Custom-build an international service experience for your educational or community group. Discounts are available for groups based on the number of volunteers.

Volunteers pay a $500 registration fee that covers accommodation and food during the project and are responsible for their own airfare. Projects in Asia, Africa, and Central and South America may have an extra fee of $200 to $500. Scholarships are available and awarded based on VFP's criteria. In order to volunteer with VFP, you need to be a US citizen.

WWOOF

Worldwide Opportunities on Organic Farms (WWOOF) is a network that connects organic farms around the world, including in the United States, with people looking to trade agricultural labor for lodging, food, and cultural exchange. WWOOF has several aims:

- give a firsthand experience of organic or other ecologically sound growing methods
- provide experience of life in the countryside
- help the organic movement, which is labor-intensive and does not rely on artificial fertilizers, herbicides, or pesticides
- give people a chance to meet, talk, learn, and exchange views with others in the organic movement
- provide an opportunity to learn about life in the host country by living and working together

Every country has its own WWOOF network, so the best way to begin is to go to the WWOOF website (wwoof.net) and pick a country. You'll be redirected to the options available in your country of choice. You'll have to pay your travel expenses to the farm you agree to work with, and depending on the location, the cost can get expensive. That being said, working on an organic dairy farm in New Zealand might be worth it. WWOOF does not provide a stipend, so if you choose this option, you might want to have some cash saved up.

US Department of State Student Internship Program

This unpaid program provides an opportunity to work in US embassies throughout the world, as well as in various bureaus located in Washington, DC, and at Department of State offices spread around the United States. According to their brochure, as an intern you might participate in meetings with senior-level US government or foreign government officials; draft, edit, or contribute to cables, reports, communications, talking points, or other materials; support events, including international or multilateral meetings and conferences; or work directly with US audiences in helping to explain the work of the Department of State or with foreign audiences to promote and explain US foreign policy and improve understanding of US culture and society.

The internship is unpaid, so you will have to bankroll your own housing, clothing, and food, and note that you must currently be a student. In return for your service, you will get an insider's view of the Department of State, the chance to work at a US embassy or consulate overseas, and some pretty remarkable references and experiences to put on your résumé. Qualifications for acceptance are

- US citizenship
- good academic standing (at least a 2.5 GPA)
- successful completion of a background investigation
- ability to receive either a public trust, secret, or top secret clearance
- drug-free lifestyle
- status as a junior or senior, or within five months of being a junior or senior. This means you have been accepted for

enrollment, or are enrolled, as a degree-seeking student in an accredited college or university and have sixty or more credit hours.

Cross-Cultural Solutions

Cross-Cultural Solutions (CCS) is a nonprofit that specializes in setting up international volunteers in different host cities around the world to assist in education, health care, agriculture, and community development projects. The approach promises to provide you with meaningful work that addresses a specific community need in the countries CCS serves: Tanzania, India, South Africa, Costa Rica, Morocco, Guatemala, Thailand, Peru, Brazil, and Ghana. Housing, meals, guidance, language lessons, and a personalized volunteer assignment are all provided (for a fee). CCS promises a fully immersive experience. But—and it's a big but—you pay quite a bit for the opportunity: a twelve-week stint can cost nearly $9,000 and a four-week expedition just over $4,000. If this sounds interesting, go to their website (crossculturalsolutions.org) and browse the comprehensive list of possible positions and destinations. There's something for everyone.

Projects Abroad

Want to teach yoga in Peru or help provide microfinancing in Senegal? Endeavors like these may be just right for you. Similar to CCS, Projects Abroad is a fee-based volunteer and internship abroad program. Internships are also available in specific training fields, such as health care, legal services, journalism, and business. Each year, more than 10,000 volunteers go abroad to provide various services in education, conservation, construction, animal care, and human rights efforts. The fee covers food, accommodation, insurance, and plenty of training. The prices are a bit less than those charged by CCS, with a four-week experience ranging from $3,000 to $3,500. You also have to pay for your own plane fare. Again, the best way to find a specific position is to browse their website (projects-abroad.org). They will help you narrow down your options by tailoring a position and destination to suit your interests.

GoEco (goeco.org)

This organization is a fee-based group and specializes in finding participants for ethical volunteer projects abroad with an ecological focus. From working with endangered sea turtles in Bali to learning about recycling and sustainability in Thailand to saving coral in Belize to caring for orphaned wildlife in Zimbabwe, GoEco has a multitude of offerings, but you have to pay to access them (anywhere from $800 to $2,000 a week). Fees provide food and housing, training, supervision, and safety precautions as well as site-specific expenses (like scuba certification if you are diving). GoEco has been sending volunteers abroad for 13 years and have placed over 17,000 volunteers across the globe. Each program has costs and itinerary spelled out, as well as a history of impact in the region.

TRY IT OUT RIGHT NOW!

You don't have to wait until you graduate to volunteer abroad. All of the organizations listed in this section have summer and teen programming. Plus, one of the most reputable groups in the country, Visions Service Adventures (visionsserviceadventures.com), has been operating for more than twenty-five years sending middle and high school students on national and international community service programs. Built on the idea of becoming a kind of Peace Corps for teens, Visions began in the early 1970s when, as the website describes, "a few New York friends and educators relocated to a rural Pennsylvania farm and established an experiential summer camp for teens. Years of summers in this setting taught us that kids loved the camaraderie, the physical labor and the shared sense of purpose. Teenagers want to be part of something bigger than themselves and are willing to work hard to meet big goals."

Where There Be Dragons (wheretherebedragons.com) is another terrific organization that offers experiences abroad, doing service and experiential learning in developing countries. The programs, as the website notes, provide "authentic, rugged, and profound student travel adventures" with extended itineraries for summer, semester-away, and gap year adventures. The kinds of students who most enjoy this program are "creative, bright, curious people in search of a more honest understanding of human relationships, environmental and social dynamics, and the meaning and value of their existence."

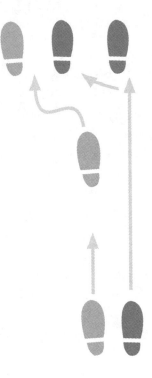

Nothing will work unless you do.

—*Maya Angelou*

part four:
work

What You Need to Know

Federal youth labor laws will allow you to work limited hours if you are fourteen or fifteen, or unlimited hours if you are sixteen or seventeen, with hazardous work being one of the few exceptions. By the time you are eighteen, all the youth restrictions are lifted, which means you can basically jump into a nine-to-five routine as soon as you stow your cap and gown and frame your high school diploma. Work is a huge part of adult life. Your mission is to figure out if now is the time to begin or if you should take advantage of the next few years to experiment with other opportunities before settling into a job.

But first things first. There's a big incentive to getting straight to work for one obvious reason: you make money. The sooner you start making money, the longer the span of years you have to grow and accumulate that income (provided you don't blow it on stuff you don't need) and the more stable and secure you can become. Age or lack of degree won't get in the way. According to the US Department of Labor, twenty-four out of the thirty fastest-growing sectors of our economy require only a high school degree or equivalent to get a job. Only three require a bachelor's degree, and the remaining three require an associate's degree. Many of these occupations are health and service oriented: nurse's aides, home health aides, phlebotomists, and medical assistants. These may not be your dream jobs, but they are paid work.

Work is a tricky subject to offer as an option, because eventually everyone has to do it. For most of us, it's not a choice. The only choices are when to start, what kind of work to do, and for how many hours, so you can make ends meet. There's also the long-term, more radical difference—the happiness quotient difference—between doing work that you love and clocking hours at a job just for cash. But at this stage of the game, the vast majority of work available to you is going to be the latter: low-priority, minimum-wage, minimal-skills-required labor. The upside to this kind of work is that you can do it and still do other things that inspire you more, like write your screenplay, refine your business plan, play music, or study. The downside is that these jobs are often physically tiring, boring, and more than a little soul sucking, which can take the wind out of your sails if you don't have a life goal that you are working toward.

If you are blessed to have parents or a benefactor willing to give you some financial breathing room over the next couple years, my best advice is to take it. Put off getting a full-time job and further your education or training in some way. If you are burning to start a business and your parents are willing to help, the same thing goes. This may be the only time in your life when you will get that breathing room, and that money should be considered an investment in you. You have the time and the energy right now to make a lot of things happen. If you have funding too, that is a recipe for real success. Success comes in all forms, not just financial, and if you have adults in your life willing to make sacrifices to support you and your dream or your art, the unspoken transaction of the generations is that someday, when you are older and more secure, you will be in a position to return their investment and faith in you by taking care of them and spending time with them.

If you need to fully support yourself, there's no reason to think that the other options outlined in this book are out of reach. They just may take more time to achieve. It is possible to hold down a thirty-hour-per-week job and take two night classes a semester at your local community college, trade school, or state university. After a couple of years, you may have saved enough money to take the time off to finish your bachelor's degree or apprenticeship elsewhere, travel, start a business, or participate in a cool service opportunity that leads to a whole new chapter of your life.

Internships and Apprenticeships

Internships and apprenticeships are a hybrid of volunteering and work. The idea behind internships and apprenticeships is that they are of mutual benefit to you and the business or trade you work for. You exchange your time and effort for the chance to learn about a specific kind of work you are likely to pursue as a career. You learn by watching and helping someone else do the work. Your employer gains by getting an extra pair of hands. Some internships and apprenticeships are unpaid, or offer a small stipend, while others are paid. It all depends on the company or organization.

Internships are most often in administrative or office work, while apprenticeships are centered on learning a trade or craft. Many internships and apprenticeships are tailored for college graduates or students enrolled in college, community college, or trade school, but this is not always the case—almost every organization that has interns is willing to make exceptions for an extraordinary candidate.

Tons of organizations offer internships and apprenticeships in exciting fields: communications, publishing, art, industrial arts, science, museums, technology, computer animation and design, public affairs, and human services. Generally, you'll find good internship programs in fields that are doing interesting, often high-minded work. You'll find apprenticeships through trade schools and community colleges.

ACING IT 101

Internships and apprenticeships begin like any other job: with an application and an interview. If you are invited to interview for a position, do a reasonable amount of research on the business before your interview date and dress with professionalism. Make sure your clothes, skin, hair, and nails are clean (you would be surprised at how many employers take personal hygiene into account during interviews) and take care to make direct eye contact with your interviewer. This is not the day for UGGs, flip-flops, or weather-beaten sneakers. Put yourself in your interviewer's place for a minute, and imagine the possible concerns they might have as a result of your relative youth and inexperience. Your job is to show them their concerns are groundless. Any employer wants all of their employees to represent the business well. The interview is the place to prove you can do that. If, later on, you find out everyone wears jeans and T-shirts, go ahead and dial down your outfit after you've landed the spot—but for that first interview, dress up.

Take a few notes during or right after the interview: write down your interviewer's name (correctly spelled) and email, the name of the front desk person (helpful when checking your status by phone), and any little details of the conversation that strike you. At all times, keep in mind that you are trying to convey why you, specifically, will add value to the business. After the interview, send a quick email thanking your interviewer for meeting with you. Follow it up with a written letter—preferably filled with observations about their company and sparkling moments of brilliance you remember from the interview.

If this sounds like a lot of sweat to get a temporary position, let me tell you why it's worth it: internships and apprenticeships are proven gateways to real employment and are considered to be the most reliable, structured path toward qualification in certain fields. They are also the most traditional form of learning. In ye olden times, the only way to learn how to do anything was to apprentice yourself to someone who was already doing it. But don't be naive about the kind of work you might be expected to do in between the cool stuff. It's the work nobody else has time to do or wants to do. Lick envelopes? Yes. Vacuum the carpet? Yes. Clean the company refrigerator? Yes. Some employers take advantage of their interns, but remember what I said earlier: the experience should be mutually beneficial. If you aren't learning anything, tell someone and ask for different responsibilities or quit.

INTERNSHIP IS NOT OWNERSHIP

Businesses love interns and apprentices because they provide help without unduly raising overhead, but this should not result in your exploitation. It is a company's responsibility to respect their interns and apprentices and implement a goals-oriented plan that is decided upon before you show up on your first day. By law, the only way employers can skirt paying you at least minimum wage is to provide you with training that could be considered of equal value to a starting, entry-level salary. Mindless copying and emptying garbage cans does not qualify (unless those tasks are part of a larger experience). If your employer does not provide you with work that expands your skills either through tasks or people, you have the right to sue. According to the Fair Labor Standards Act, there are six criteria that companies must meet in order to employ temporary, unpaid interns (rather than entry-level employees):

- The internship must be similar to training that would be provided in an educational environment
- The experience is for the benefit of the intern
- The intern does not displace regular employees but is supervised by existing staff
- The employer providing the training derives no immediate advantage from the activities of the intern; and on occasion its operations may actually be impeded
- The intern is not necessarily entitled to a job after completion of internship
- The employer and the intern both understand the intern is unpaid

If all of these criteria are met, the relationship is not officially one between an employer-employee but more like teacher-student. Getting all these criteria right can be difficult for businesses (after

✔ Making Internships Work

Legendary publisher Condé-Nast announced the end of its historic internship program in 2014 due to pending lawsuits filed by low-paid or unpaid interns claiming the company violated minimum-wage laws. Hearst Magazines, Fox Searchlight Pictures, Madison Square Garden, and Donna Karan have also been sued by low-paid or unpaid interns for the same reason. In the case against Karan, a twenty-five-year-old man claims he worked 16 hours a week without pay in exchange for the "learning" experience of fetching coffee and organizing closets. Not exactly the educational experience prescribed by the FLSA. So know your rights and don't be a doormat, but also don't be confused about what an internship is. You will have to do menial jobs; you will be paid nothing or very little; and you will be the lowest person on the totem pole. In return, however, you must receive exposure to people and skills that expand your understanding of the profession and build your résumé. If it is not a hands-on, educational experience, then it's time for you to leave.

all, it is in the nature of business to try to gain advantage from your work), but there are plenty out there that have a good history of working with interns. A great place to start researching internships is at internships.com or idealist.org. Both have internship listings, as does mediabistro.com. Wayup.com provides a searchable database of reputable internships by location and interest, and they have great organizational tools to help you land the internship in the field you really want.

OTHER PLACES TO LOOK

Your first stop should be your high school guidance counselor's office. It is common for businesses to keep a running dialogue with local high schools because they are a great source of untapped labor. If in previous years students and businesses had good experiences, there is an excellent chance that your guidance counselor can serve as a pipeline into these businesses and help you land a place. Some schools, like Portland High School in Maine, where I live, are creating a career-focused curriculum in conjunction with local business leaders. Sophomores at PHS are now required to participate in a program that has job shadowing as part of the school day. The goal is to break down the invisible line that separates school from the world of work, and to help students find direction and work opportunities after they graduate.

USAJOBS.gov will direct you to the Office of Personnel Management, otherwise known as the HR department of the Feds. It offers a new internship program replacing all the other student programs formerly in use. Each agency is responsible for hiring their own interns at their own discretion, so if being in DC at the center of the drama is what you want, you will need to look closely at the role of each federal agency, know who the current director is (they change frequently nowadays), and decide if that's where you want to apply. Applicants for these internships must be US citizens and one of the following:

- Currently enrolled in an accredited high school; college (including four-year colleges and universities, community colleges, and junior colleges); professional, technical, vocational,

When considering an internship or apprenticeship, ask yourself the following questions:

- What kind of work or trade am I most interested in learning how to do?
- Who do I want to work with?
- Where do I want to work?
- How much time am I willing to spend in an internship or apprenticeship?
- What do I hope to get out of an internship or apprenticeship?
- Do I want to go to school while I intern?
- How flexible do I need my internship or apprenticeship to be?
- Am I willing to compete for an internship or apprenticeship placement?
- How far am I willing to travel for my internship or apprenticeship?

Some internship programs offer a lot of flexibility; others are more rigid and require a real commitment. Some offer four- or twelve-week stints; others want you for a whole summer or a full year. And some are in high demand and very competitive to get. Then there are the old-school internships and apprenticeships that you can get simply by walking into a business or studio you like and asking if the owner needs free help.

(If you do this, it might make sense to go back and reread the previous sections about getting value for your labor—just to make sure you know what you are getting into.)

or trade school; advanced degree program; or other qualifying educational institution and pursuing a qualifying degree or certificate

- Graduated from an undergraduate or graduate program at a college, community college, or university (two- to four-year institution) no more than two years before the first day of the internship
- A veteran of the US armed forces who possesses a high school diploma or its equivalent and has served on active duty, for any length of time, in the two years preceding the first day of the internship

Federal interns may be hired temporarily or indefinitely, and it's possible for the internship to convert to a permanent position based on certain criteria and hours worked. Most of the requirements are agency-specific.

You can also hire professionals. The Center of Interim Programs (interimprograms.com), founded by the legendary educator Cornelius Bull, is now managed by his daughter, Holly. Since 1980 the center has been matching clients with work that suits their interests all across the world. As the mission states, the center provides structured alternatives to education and work—something your parents will appreciate! This is a service, so you will have to pay, but finding you a terrific internship or apprenticeship could be the first step in a career that will more than return that initial investment. How about an internship in wildlife rescue and management? Or an apprenticeship in art restoration in France? Or a journalism internship in Chicago? This is the kind of exploration I'm talking about.

If you are interested in learning a skilled trade but aren't psyched about trade school, you can look for salaried apprenticeships in

profile

Blake Mycoskie, cobbler, founder, chief shoe-giver at Toms

Blake Mycoskie was born in Texas in 1976, the son of an orthopedic surgeon and a cookbook author. He never graduated from high school (he didn't complete his Spanish requirement) but got recruited to play tennis at Southern Methodist University anyway. It didn't stick, and he dropped out after two years as a philosophy and business major. An avid reader, he spent his own time learning a lot about business and philanthropy through books, but he didn't have much hands-on experience when he started his first of six successful companies: a door-to-door laundry company called EZ Laundry. He went on to found a billboard company that got bought out by Clear Channel, a reality TV cable channel, and an online driver-training company before he was inspired to create Toms Shoes in 2006. His eureka moment came while traveling in Argentina, where he met a woman who was collecting shoes for the poor. In the spring of 2019, Toms gave away its 95 millionth pair of shoes as part of the company's mission to give away one pair for every pair sold.

skilled labor at apprenticeship.gov. This national search tool will link you to paid training and apprenticeships in your area. The only requirement is that you are sixteen years of age or older (eighteen if you are interested in hazardous work) and physically able to do the work. Through this program, you are promised a paycheck from day one that will increase as training progresses, and a combination of targeted education and hands-on training that eventually gets you a nationally recognized certification.

Starting a Business

C onsider this quote from PayPal founder Peter Thiel:

> I think anything that requires real global
> breakthroughs requires a degree of intensity and
> sustained effort that cannot be done part time,
> so it's something you have to do around the
> clock, and that doesn't compute with our existing
> educational system.

Thiel put his money where his mouth is and started a foundation
in 2000 that pays twenty young, bright, innovative people each
year *not* to go to college. The program, 20 under 20, now the Thiel
Foundation, gives $100,000 to each fellow in exchange for moving to
San Francisco for two years to launch a high-tech business. During that

time, the fellows are not allowed to go to school or work and instead must focus entirely on creating the next best new thing. In Thiel's opinion, the money most people spend on college tuition would be better invested in ideas that could be the breakthroughs of the future and in people who may become the business leaders of the future.

You don't have to become a Thiel fellow to start your own business right after high school (although if you have a radical new idea, go for it and apply at thielfellowship.org). But you do need to have an idea or skill you can market and some kind of business plan to follow. Succeeding at a small business is notoriously hard. Nine out of ten new businesses fail—and a good scenario is just breaking even. Once in a while, entrepreneurs strike gold, and you will be much more motivated to dig deep if you are building your own business rather than working for someone else's. You will have to make sacrifices, such as living at home, taking on debt, working another job, or forgoing your social life, until your business gets on its feet.

So how do you know if starting a business is the best plan for you? The first thing to do is to go back to part one and look at the interests you checked on pages 40–41. Does the list have a unifying theme or include a marketable skill? Can you think of a realistic way to turn any of those interests into a business? (For instance, playing with your dog could become a pet-sitting business.) Alternatively, do you have a good idea that you think could make money? Don't be afraid to consider something obvious. Paul Orfalea, the founder of Kinko's (see page 38), got the idea for his business by watching the long lines of students waiting for the copier at the University of Southern California library. If so, begin writing a business plan so you can get a loan. Ask yourself the following questions:

- Is your idea original?
- Is there relatively little competition in your area?
- Can you articulate your idea in a business plan or find similar business models?
- Are you passionate enough about your idea to spend most of your waking hours working on it?
- Could you partner with someone?
- Is there a measurable market for your idea?
- Are there people around you who can help you solve problems?
- Do you have help underwriting your business?
- Is there something about you that makes you the best person for this business?

If you answered yes to these questions, your idea just might have the makings of a start-up. At the very least, your business idea deserves serious discussion. And don't wait. Early to mid-twenties seems to be the magic age for launching a business, and no age is too young to begin your business experience. Lots of successful business leaders got their start with humble beginnings. Elon Musk, the founder of Tesla Motors and cofounder of PayPal, initially made money by writing video games. Virgin empire wunderkind Richard Branson hawked Christmas trees. Mark Cuban, owner of the NBA Dallas Mavericks, sold garbage bags.

IS IT GONNA WORK?

That is the key question, of course. And who knows, really? But before you go sinking a ton of time and money, bring out the old pencil and paper and write up a business plan. At the very least, this is a good way to lay all your ideas out on paper and give them a once-over. At best, it will be the beginning of your pitch to future investors. If at the end of writing it all down, your idea loses steam, don't worry. Go back through the pages of this book, and find some existing opportunities that might be a good complement to your idea (if we stick with the dog-walking business hypothesis, you might get an internship or part-time job at an animal shelter or vet). Working in a related field could end up giving you insight into a different way to make your idea pop or create connections with potential customers. A few good websites can help you write up a finished business plan, including Score.org and SBA.gov. In the meantime, any theoretical business plan should answer the following questions:

- What is the name of my business?
- Where is my business (address, website, contact info)?
- What is the mission or purpose of my business?
- What services will my business provide?
- Who will buy or support the services of my business and why?
- Who are my competitors?
- How will I market my business?
- Who will help me start my business (advisers and investors)?
- What kind of business is my business, legally (LLC, incorporated, nonprofit, etc.)?
- Who will work with me at my business (staff)?
- What will their roles be?
- How much will I pay them?
- What are the personal values I want my business to reflect?
- What are my short-term goals for this business?

- What are my long-term goals for this business?

And then—of course—you have to deal with the financials. Use the very basic business budget worksheet below to get a better idea of your expenses.

Expenses		Funding	
Registration and Licenses	$	Investors/Seed Money	$
Legal Fees	$	Savings	$
Equipment	$	Gifts	$
Staff	$	Partner	$
Rentals (Space and Vehicle)	$	Loans	$
Website	$	Grants	$
Supplies	$	Projected Sales Income	$
Advertising	$	Monthly	$
Salaries	$	Annually	$
Insurance and Taxes	$	Other	$

My first-year expenses will be $_____

My first-year income will be $_____

FIND SOME HELP

One of the best places to look when you are thinking about going out on your own is inwardly, toward your obsessions. Is there something you love to do to the exclusion of everything else? Is there a problem that keeps you up at night thinking of cool ways to solve it? Maybe you can't stop focusing on a new mobile app or a T-shirt design or how to build a solar panel or kayak. If there is something, you might be able to get paid for it (eventually) after a lot of hard work. This is the stuff of true job satisfaction, because the best work is work that doesn't feel like work. So, if you have a real passion or obsession, reread chapter 15 on internships and apprenticeships. Then go online and research people you admire who are already doing what you love professionally (or something similar), and write to them. Ask for advice, maybe even a job or an apprenticeship. Once you learn the ropes, you will know how—and if—you can make it on your own. This is called mentoring, and almost no one succeeds in a professional capacity without it. Education, in college, vocational school, or a certification program, is another way to access mentors.

You can find lots of resources for building a small business that will guide you (and your folks) step-by-step through the basics. *The Young Entrepreneur's Guide to Starting and Running a Business: Turn Your Ideas into Money!* by Steve Mariotti offers real-life stories and a bible on how to do it yourself. And if you want a little sizzle, you could get the good word on building a business from Richard Branson in his book *Screw It, Let's Do It.* Stop by your local chamber of commerce. Chambers have general and regional-specific information you can use. Go online and check out the money making ideas, guides, and start-up information at these sites:

- SBA.gov (US Small Business Administration)
- Inc.com
- Entrepreneur.com
- JuniorBiz.com

Getting a Job

Mighty oaks spring from tiny acorns, and so it is true that most adults started out at your age by working minimum-wage day jobs that required no skills and no experience to get. Some of us cringe when we remember those jobs, some of us look back with fondness and gratitude for the experience, and for some of us, it is a mix of both. Any job—no matter how gross—has a nugget of sweetness, even if it is simply that it motivates you to push hard to break out of it. And for the lucky ones, these first jobs are the cradle that rocks us into our future. So don't get down on yourself about working a day job. Make the most of it. And if you are doing it to support your family or yourself, or to finance a different dream, more power to you. That's the stuff of character. Award-winning actor George Clooney sold men's suits and cut tobacco before becoming famous. Brad Pitt wore a chicken costume to advertise a local restaurant in LA, and Ralph Lauren worked the floor at Brooks Brothers. Working a day job lays down a good foundation for any future.

Day jobs generally pay by the hour and exist all around you, in every store, restaurant, retail establishment, mall, and entertainment complex across the nation. These do not necessarily require any prior experience—that's why they're called entry-level jobs. You just have to be willing to do the grunt work. In high school, I worked the following day jobs in no particular order: babysitting, scooping ice cream, washing dishes, retail sales, aiding a catering company, baking cakes for a café, and checking out and bagging groceries at a natural food store. None of these jobs paid more than minimum wage, and most (except babysitting) were an exercise in looking busy in between customers. I lost money baking cakes, and washing dishes was by far the worst job I ever had. But nonetheless, all these jobs had their benefits. I grew my people skills bagging groceries, used math skills closing out a register, and was exposed to all kinds of different managerial styles and unforeseen learning opportunities.

Making your own money, even a small amount, will buy you so many more choices in life. It is the seed of independence, the jet fuel for your rocket into adulthood. So whether or not you plan to go straight to work after high school, it's a good idea to get some kind of hourly job as soon as you can (age sixteen, or fourteen with a parent's permission), part time or during the summer. If you need to work full time or part time after you graduate to support yourself, having previous work experience and references can only help you land a better position and better shifts. Work is going to be part of

A day job will teach you many things:

- How to apply for and land a job
- How to work for a boss
- How fast a reliable, energetic person can gain responsibility and status
- How to work with the public
- How to show up when you say you will
- How independent you can be with a regular paycheck
- How to complete tasks that you don't like
- How easy it is to make money if you work hard
- How one job leads to another leads to another
- How a bad job can tell you a lot about what you really want to do with your life
- How to quit responsibly

almost any equation after high school, but the best part about a day job is that it is usually temporary. It serves a purpose. And at your age, quitting these kinds of jobs is easy, especially if you are using your earnings to study or follow other dreams.

WORK TOWARD A GOAL

Working a day job is a responsible way to support yourself or the means to a different end, especially if you've gone through this book and figured out a more inspiring plan you want to achieve (eventually). Once you've done that and zeroed in on the specific schools or programs you want to apply to, calculate how much money you will need to make the plan work (see page 216). Then calculate how many hours you will have to work at minimum wage—in 2020 the federal minimum wage is still (yes, still) $7.25 an hour, although some states have higher and some have lower minimum wages for certain workers and some don't have a minimum wage law at all—to achieve that sum. (Don't forget that taxes and federal deductions will be taken out of your paycheck. To see what that looks like in real time, go to smartasset.com/taxes/paycheck-calculator and enter your data.) If you are using your day job to support yourself while you pursue other (unpaid) passions, know that you are already in the process of achieving your goal.

THE BASICS

What

You'll need the following to apply for and get a day job:

- A résumé and a list of references and their contact information for applications
- A social security number and tax identification number
- Proof of legal citizenship and age
- A stable living situation so you can focus on work or your internship or apprenticeship
- Reliable transportation or transportation plan
- A working phone, an email account, or both so potential employers can contact you
- A copy of your high school transcript and diploma to keep on file in case you want to apply for more training or education in the future

A résumé is, in plain English, a list of stuff you've done. But trust me, unless you are Mozart, it is not going to sizzle at this stage of the game. What you can do is make a nice, neat list of all the activities and any work (paid or volunteer) you've done so far. Word-processing software generally has a résumé template built in that you can use, or go to GCFGlobal (edu.gcfglobal.org) and follow their tips. Just remember that a lot of résumé advice is geared to experienced workers. Take it easy on yourself, and follow these basic rules:

- Be truthful (it is tempting to pad your experience, but don't).
- Be organized (format information in an easy-to-read, consistent way).
- Be available and reachable (put your contact info front and center, and answer calls).
- Don't forget school-based activities and clubs.

If you have done absolutely nothing up until now, don't worry. Plenty of day jobs require nothing more than your contact info and a list of personal references on a standard application, but even your local café or pizza joint might ask you for a résumé. Don't stress too much about this. It's often just a formality and only needs to be a sheet of paper with your contact info, your job experience—even if it's just mowing the lawn and babysitting once for your cousin—and your references contact info. If you want to build your résumé, go to chapter 23 and read about different volunteer opportunities right in your backyard that might give you a leg up. It's not hard, I promise. You just have to do something. It will lead to other things, which will lead to a robust résumé down the road.

- Take a walk in your neighborhood, and look in store and restaurant windows. Chances are, you will see a "help wanted" sign.
- Sign up for Indeed, Idealist, or Monster to get job alerts in your zip code.
- Ask your friends who already have jobs if there is an opening where they work.
- Look on bulletin boards at local cafés, coffee shops, and laundromats (but don't go to personal interviews alone without checking out the source).
- Ask your parents, relatives, and their friends to be alert for job openings.
- Talk to your guidance counselor at school and let them know. They will have contacts in your town who have hired kids just like you.

No one expects you to have any previous experience at this point. Don't be intimidated by a standard job application. Just fill it out and leave it with the manager. These entry-level jobs have high turnover rates, so chances are you will hear of an opening soon if you get out there.

If you need more ideas, here are some that are available to a high school graduate (or anyone over sixteen) with no previous experience or training, culled from Harlow G. Unger's excellent reference book *But What If I Don't Want to Go to College?* To get ahead in any of these fields—in other words, move up to management—you will need more on-the-job experience and often some kind of certification or training, but you have to start somewhere:

- Agriculture or farmwork
- Amusement park attendant
- Arts: performance, photography
- Baker
- Barista
- Childcare
- Clerical support
- Construction
- Customer service
- Floral designer
- Forestry service
- Graphic design assistant
- Grocery worker
- Hospitality
- Housekeeping and cleaning
- Kitchen and food and beverage service
- Landscaping, gardening, and plant nursery
- Lifeguard or assistant coach
- Personal assistant
- Retail sales
- Theater usher or ticket taker

You can also apply to work for the government as a postal clerk or mail carrier, school crossing guard, firefighter, corrections officer, police worker, teachers' assistant, or EMT—but not right away. Government jobs usually require a high school diploma, six months' experience, and passing the appropriate service exam and physical fitness requirements.

And one last thing about looking for a job: Don't just take the first job you can find, unless you are flat-out busted broke. Go back to the first section, and revisit all the work you did learning about yourself and your dreams. Search for a reasonable job that has something to do with what you like or at least suits your temperament. If you are an extroverted party person, you are not going to like a job that keeps you disconnected and in isolation, like

looking back

"In 2010 I moved to Portland [Maine] to be a student in the Salt Institute for Documentary Studies semester-long radio program. Following the semester I took a job as a customer service associate at Whole Foods Market to pay the bills. After six or seven months I yearned to feel creative in my work and advance my career. I looked into jobs and found an AmeriCorps position at the Telling Room, a nonprofit writing center for kids. The position was for a volunteer and program assistant. I applied for the job and got it after a competitive interview process. I also began training and coordinating a corps of over three hundred volunteers. I had taught in the past, but had never managed and overseen a group of adults in the way the volunteer coordinator job required. I learned on the job and also found a lot of support from my peers in the AmeriCorps group—many of whom were also coordinating volunteers.

"Over the course of my two years at the Telling Room, my management and leadership skills grew immensely. I became a confident professional. My employers noticed my talent in multimedia and allowed me to start new programs in documentary studies and also begin a podcast. Toward the end of my second term, the Telling Room was financially secure enough to offer me a job as director of multimedia, having created the job description around my strengths and talents."

—M. Haley, photographer

shelving books or working the night shift at a laundromat. You'd be much better off using your social skills in retail sales or in a restaurant. If you go against your grain, there's a real chance you'll end up quitting after only a few days, which means you won't get a good reference. If you can, stay at a day job at least for a summer or a six-month period before switching; that way it doesn't look like you're job-hopping. Employers value reliability.

Working a Job

You got the job. Your first shift is tomorrow. What do you need to know to start off on the right foot?

Work is not school. Yes, you will learn from a good employer, but they have no obligation to cut you slack, understand your personal life, give you a second chance or encouragement, or see to it that you are having a good experience that makes you a better person. You have been hired to perform a series of tasks, and the only reward you are legally obligated to receive is your paycheck.

Show up and be on time. Part of the job is being there for the agreed-upon amount of time, not five minutes late or tomorrow or calling in with a thin excuse ("My allergies are acting up—can't make it today").

Be prompt. Once you have an understanding of your shift or days, do a dry-run commute at the same time you will be doing it for real. Plan for traffic and congestion ahead of time. If parking is an issue, ask your employer about better places to park or use public transportation. If you find that you don't want to be there after all, quit gracefully with some notice. Don't just bail. If you do it right, you might be able to get a recommendation from your employer even if you haven't worked there long.

Understand the chain of command. Know from the outset to whom you are supposed to report directly and, in turn, to whom that person reports. Be straightforward and clear about who is supposed to give you orders and who isn't. This becomes very important if things go wrong, since you will probably be the lowest person on the totem pole and the easiest to fire.

Look the part. Save your super-creative fashion expression for outside of work, and comply with the accepted dress code of the company. This is easy if you have a uniform. If not, check the employee handbook or ask a manager before your first shift. If you still aren't sure, check out how your fellow employees are clad (including their shoes, because it is torture being on your feet all day in uncomfortable shoes). Pick out a few go-to outfits. This will help save time in the morning too.

Play by the rules. Once you've been trained, do things by the book or take extra time to develop an alternative system and present it to your employer. Don't be a maverick at this stage (you are trying to go places from here). If you have an idea, show your employer why it is more efficient and should be adopted. If your employer is convinced, make a note of this for your next review. If your idea is rejected, let it go and save it for later—maybe when you start your own business.

Ask for regular reviews. These are standard fare in the adult universe and obligatory in most administrative and business professions. A regular or annual performance review will give your boss a chance to discuss your strengths and weaknesses in your job, set goals, and brainstorm your trajectory. It gives you a chance to promote or defend yourself, ask for a raise, and set your own goals and trajectory. Throughout the years, keep track of extra work and any additional value you've contributed to the business, and where you see yourself going in the company. Bring all of this to your annual review.

Set goals. The most obvious way to enjoy your day job is to do it in service of something larger, whether that thing is funding a trip, getting into a better school, helping your family financially, or buying a new car. One of the most satisfying things about working a day job is that the more hours you work, the more you get paid, so you can be somewhat in control of how much you make. This is different from a salary, which is set ahead of time on an annual or monthly basis, regardless of actual "worked" hours. Goals don't have to be material, either. It will always serve you well to set a goal to work efficiently and to the best of your ability. Pay attention to detail. Learn what the boss needs. Be trustworthy and think of creative solutions to problems (there is always room for creativity—even in the worst jobs). If you set your own bar high, you will be amazed at how quickly you can rise into a manager spot.

looking back

"My direction in life presented itself early, and by the age of fifteen, I was deeply involved in extensive musical studies. I left high school early in my sophomore year to have my time free to study and practice, and I moved away from home soon afterward. I was able to support myself working in music stores and record stores, and this not only provided income but fed back into my musical pursuits as I was exposed to many genres of music and became familiar with much that would have otherwise remained hard to come by. It was at these job positions that I learned important people skills and how to use my time more effectively. I had to learn to accept criticism from supervisors and how to think critically about the tasks I was assigned and how to carry them out efficiently. I was responsible for my own transportation to and from work and for getting myself to work on time. I also had to learn budgeting for my daily needs and rent. The drawback to working a job of that type is that it took up time that I would have preferred to use playing and studying. I had to learn to push through the times when boredom threatened to set in and develop good work habits and focus. To be able to afford rent and expenses, I worked full-time hours. A job of that kind certainly increases appreciation for days off and free time and one becomes adept at using free time productively."

—J. McCain, musician, artist, and teacher

Self-discipline and inner motivation are two pretty obvious qualities that most good employers will reward. However, if you are working fifty hours at the local gelato shop, doing your best to be the best gelato purveyor you can be, and you aren't feeling any love, one of the most important goals to set is when and in what graceful manner you will eventually quit.

Know when a job isn't working out. This is probably the hardest thing to grapple with. You get paid to work because it's often hard, boring, political, or repetitive. Often it can be fun and interesting too, and a good job will be bearable or even enjoyable, despite its challenges. If, however, your job is making you consistently miserable, if your boss is abusive or discriminatory, if you aren't making enough money to support yourself, or if you are suffering health problems because of work, know that it is time to blow this particular popsicle stand. Don't fret too much about it. People quit all the time. But before you lay down the hammer, put out feelers for another opportunity. Check into college classes or a volunteer program that might form a good exit strategy. Then be honest and give your employer the option of two weeks' notice.

If you get fired: Ask for an exit interview to find out the reasons why you have been fired. If the reason is not poor performance, ask for a reference or recommendation from your boss. If your firing is performance-based, ask what you could have done differently. If you have been getting regular reviews, you probably will know already. If not, an honest reply is the least your ex-employer should give you—so ask. Know that if you are fired, you may be eligible for unemployment, depending on how long you have worked and how many hours. If you sign a private employment contract, be sure to read the dismissal clauses carefully so that you understand the reasons why you could be dismissed, in what manner, and with how much warning.

You have a right to be treated fairly and equally as an employee under Title VII of the Civil Rights Act of 1964. *For now.* As I write this, several challenges to Title VII protections are under review by the Supreme Court and things may have changed by the time you read this.

Title VII of the Civil Rights Act of 1964, along with other acts passed since, state that it is illegal to discriminate against a job applicant or an employee because of the person's race, color, religion, sex (including pregnancy, gender identity, and sexual orientation), national origin, age (40 or older), disability, or genetic information. It is also illegal to discriminate against a person because the person complained about discrimination, filed a charge of discrimination, or participated in an employment discrimination investigation or lawsuit. Not only is it illegal, but in this day and age of social media, it's also shortsighted. But that doesn't mean employers won't try, and if empowered by a conservative court ruling, they may succeed. The good news is that many states will still offer protections, so keep an eye on your state legislature. If you feel discriminated against or harassed by an employer, you can file an Equal Employment Opportunity Commission (EEOC) complaint through the public portal at publicportal.eeoc.gov. If you are an intern or an independent contractor, it is up to your state whether or not they extend these protections to "temporary" workers.

But let me just call it as I see it: you should not put up with a boss who makes you feel threatened or harassed. Period. You have your whole life ahead of you. It's not worth the aggravation, humiliation, and shame to put up with a boss who is a bigot, creep, or jerk. Quit.

OSHA AND YOUR SAFETY

OSHA stands for the Occupational Safety and Health Administration, established in 1971, which assures "safe and healthful working conditions for working men and women." This document overrides any private employee contract you may sign that spells out terms of your employment. OSHA exists only to protect your safety and gives workers the right to file complaints and request inspections if they feel their workplace is unsafe. It dictates a set of standards for workplaces to follow and also allows workers the legal right to receive information about hazards and methods to prevent injury. To read the act in its entirety, you can go to OSHA. gov, but many workplaces are required to display OSHA in a public place in such a manner that employees have access and can read it at will.

In addition to safety, you, as a skilled trade worker, have the right to work in a nondiscriminatory environment, free from harassment and abuse. You have the right to negotiate employment terms that spell out how many hours you will work and for how much pay, including adequate breaks in the day for meals and bathroom, plus days off, overtime, bonuses, sick days, personal days, and vacation days. If you get a job that has a union or a guild, those organizations will have negotiated the contract and, should you join the union, you will be subject to their agreed-upon terms.

For more information on your rights as a union employee, go to aflcio.org.

Looking Back

"Two weeks before I received my high school acceptance letters, my dad died. It all seemed to happen very fast—things seemed to blur together, and it was hard to keep things straight. But what I do remember is how everything was suddenly filtered through this overwhelming sense of emptiness and quiet. Everything I had worked so hard for in school seemed inconsequential, and I was forced to switch my focus from the business of being a teenager to just keeping a hold on a world that was rapidly slipping away from my mother and me.

"A couple of weeks before my first day of high school, I began experiencing excruciating stomach pains. They left me curled on the floor for hours and incapacitated me for days. School became even more impossible and the straight As that had landed me a spot in a scholar program quickly turned into Ds and Fs. Not only did my grades suffer, so did my emotional well-being. I became the invisible girl.

"By the end of the school year my gallbladder had been removed, my relationship with my mother had completely degenerated, and I was no longer able to cope. I dropped out of high school and moved out of my mother's house. Luckily, my grandfather offered me my own apartment, and at the age of fifteen I was suddenly living alone and fending for myself. I found a job at Starbucks and began earning a paycheck. As I worked I began to heal and the following semester I enrolled at a local community college. I put my nose down, I found professors and friends that believed in me, and I became the editor-in-chief of my college's newspaper. Two and a half years later I was accepted at Columbia University. The rest, as they say, is history!"

—*Ally Covino, grad student, aspiring poet*

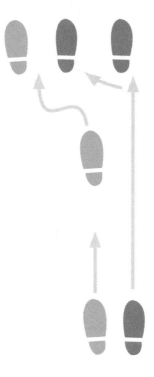

Formal education will make you a living;
self-education will make you a fortune.

—*Jim Rohn*

part five:
taking
time off

What You Need to Know

In a nutshell, this section is what this book is all about: getting off the beaten track and taking some time to experiment with the unknown. In other words, making space in your life to get a life—not slaving away at other people's expectations of you. I've spent a lot of time thinking about what that expression—"get a life"—means for someone in high school who is looking out on the wide-open vista of the future. Like most things in life, the explanation I've found is circular. It goes back to the beginning of this book. Getting a life that makes you feel alive means knowing yourself and putting yourself out there in the world as you are now, even if you have no idea where you will end up. Our education system likes to plow kids into rows by the end of high school: you end up labeled as a scholar or a slacker or a worker, or in some cases a soldier or an athlete. Often this happens because there is little continuity between what teens experience in classrooms and what they encounter in the real world and because so much of their sense of themselves comes from what they are being told by others—overtly, with compliments and awards and grades (or lack thereof), and covertly, with media and peer pressure and relationships.

Until recently, considering taking time off was the road less traveled. In one big COVID-19 swipe, it has become a major highway. I hope after reading this far you have a better sense of what truly interests you, and the confidence in yourself to know that you can make it happen. If you still don't, there is no better time to figure it out. Take some time before college or a job and have an adventure. Experiment a little. Test yourself. The way to get a life is to get off the couch and start living, right now, in whatever mixed-up, wacky fashion you can finance or finagle: make juice out of a food truck, practice yoga, volunteer for a political campaign, enroll in a painting class, work on a farm, join a mushroom foraging club, study monkeys in Asia, babysit in Norway, write a blog, learn Portuguese online, or make T-shirts and sell them at outdoor festivals. It doesn't matter what it is—just try it. Or try all of it! You may have to socially distance or keep your travel domestic for a while, but there are no limits to your creativity.

A voice inside your head may be saying you aren't good enough, brave enough, smart enough, rich enough, or old enough yet to risk it out there—but that voice is wrong. It comes from a primitive sense of fear, a source meant to keep you safe within the confines of your known environment. It's a voice everyone hears on the brink of a new challenge, and it is the single biggest hurdle to actually achieving your most authentic life. The fact is, human beings prefer the status quo—the existing and comfortable state of affairs—but comfort can quickly become stagnation. Chaos and change is where creativity and energy thrive. And the honest-to-god truth about living is that if you don't challenge yourself to new experiences, challenges will present themselves anyway, and often not in desirable ways.

SEIZE THE DAY

There is no right answer or proper path into adulthood; there's only you and what you do. The downturn in the economy in 2008 and 2020, along with rising income inequality in the US, means that making money has become a top priority for many people, above and beyond advancing more aspirational goals like art, public discourse, social justice, peace, equality, liberty, fairness, and the pursuit of happiness. Because you have a lot of time and energy and relatively few expenses right now, you are at the perfect stage to upend that equation for a little while and blow the roof off your own life. If the COVID-19 pandemic taught us anything, it is that nothing is certain and time is precious. So, do some crazy and longed-for stuff that makes you no money but fills you with joy and a sense of competency. When you come back to the mainstream, you may find yourself all the more ready to study or work hard, and hopefully you'll have learned some bread-and-butter skills that will help keep a roof over your head.

So don't be afraid to shake it up a little after graduation. Take some time to find yourself. Call it what you want: time off, time on, time-out, finding yourself, a gap year, a bridge year, a year of living dangerously, or a Wanderjahr. But make it worthwhile. Learn something new. Travel. Do something strange. Risk something big. All of the options explored up to this point can be mixed and matched (with the exception of the military, which does its own mixing and matching within its prescribed protocols) and experimented with. Be brave enough to break out of the usual barriers, and think outside of the box.

One word to the wise: If you think that you want to attend college (four-year or two-year) at some point in the near future, apply and get in somewhere while you are still in high school so you retain your student status. It is way less hassle than applying later, and it will help you be eligible for more discounts and programs. Plus, as a current high school student, you are already on the conveyor belt of education and have all the necessary tests, transcripts, teacher recommendations, and counseling at your fingertips—and your studies are fresh in your mind. Imagine taking a couple of years off and then going back to your old high school to chase down your past teachers for letters and transcripts or having to retake the SAT. It's not the end of the world if you don't apply now, but it is much easier to be accepted first and then defer for a year or two. Very few colleges will ding you or rescind their acceptance if you defer, and most have a stated deferral policy that you can ask about before you apply. In fact, many schools appreciate it when students take time off in between high school and college (or during college) to do something interesting, if only because students return more mature and ready to learn. If you know you want to take time off after graduation, you can ask what their deferment policy is ahead of time. If they don't have one, find a school that does.

If you aren't planning on college or don't get into any of the colleges you applied to, take it as a message from the universe to strike out for territories unknown. Invent your own hybrid of work, study, and travel, or work with your parents and an expert to help you create a one-of-a-kind experience. It doesn't have to be expensive. You can work a day job and study Spanish online, then go to Peru when you've saved enough money.

Know in your bones that you are at an age when a little extra time spent in the right way (or even the slightly wrong way) is not going to ruin your endgame. Instead, it will probably sharpen your focus and improve the outcome in the long run. That's the dirty little secret most adults don't want to share: no one knows what the future holds. Not you. Not me. Not your teachers or parents or those senior college admission officers. You can make certain choices that shrink the odds, but it's all still a crapshoot. Do the best, most expansive thing you can do with what you have going on right now. Your parents may need some convincing in regard to finances and your safety. Your teachers or coaches may worry you'll fall off track. Your peers may happily shoulder their backpacks and head off to freshman psych class in the fall feeling concerned about you. But don't let any of this rock you. If what you do with your time is not stupid or criminal, move forward with the certainty that someday you are going to be like everybody else. Just not right now.

So, go ahead. There's a big world waiting.

looking back

"If I could go back and give my eighteen-year-old self advice, I'd tell her to pay close attention to her instincts about what truly interested her and then find a mentor to help her navigate a way to do it. I'd also encourage her not to worry so much about certain stuff like boyfriends and other people's opinions. When you are immersed in the culture of your family and friends, it feels like the only thing that's real, but it's not."

*—J. Andes, MSW, PhD, who went to state college for
a year and a half, dropped out to work, took courses
at community college, then went back to college*

Traveling

There is nothing like the possibility of travel to make the days pass quickly while working a crummy job. Dreams of India or Indonesia or Australia or Spain are enough for anyone to want to take time off and see the world. But there is no time like the present for you. Travel at your age is cheaper and more flexible and can be fully transformative. I still think about a boy I met in Scotland. His name was Norman, and he was from Dublin, Ireland. He had black hair and green eyes, and we fell in love on the night train from London to Ayr. If friends hadn't been waiting for me at my destination (this was before cell phones), I would have gotten off the train and stayed with him forever. Who knows? I could be writing this for you from Ireland if I had. That's my story. If you decide to travel, you will have many stories of your own.

When I was a traveling teenager (my parents called it "bumming around"), Europe was the usual destination. Nowadays, with the right guides and preparation, there is practically no corner of the planet that you can't get to and explore aside from truly dangerous areas like war zones and territories ruled by drug cartels and sex traffickers.

PAYING FOR IT

If traveling is what you want to do with your time off, the obvious next questions are where and for how long? Answering both will help you understand how much money you will need for basic travel arrangements and accommodations. Once you know this, you can zero in on sources of income. If you have parental (or some other) backing, good for you; if not, you'll have to work and save money first. But no biggie. Almost every independent "time-off" travel experience, even one you hire someone to plan, starts with a job that earns you money for travel. So set a time frame, get a day job where you can rack up the hours, and cut back your spending until you save enough to go. Alternatively, you can go back to part three and check out some of the service options, which are less expensive ways to get out of town and often provide free room and board.

Airfare is usually the greatest expense. Once you put your pin on the map, go to one of the online discount travel sites, such as Kayak, Hipmunk, Hopper, Google Flights, or Expedia. Design your round trip, and set a fare alert to notify you when prices get within your affordability range. Once you arrive at the destination, travel within the country or continent is generally cheaper, and you can usually get student discounts for train and bus fare. In Europe, travelers under age twenty-five are eligible for a youth rate of 35 percent off a second-class Eurail adult ticket. Be sure to check for travel and pandemic restrictions before booking.

Depending on where you are going, Eurail offers country hoppers a Global Pass or Youth Pass that has the added bonus of discounts on buses and boat travel. The UK, the US, Australia, Scandinavia, and Japan all have excellent rail systems and discounts for students (see ACPRail.com for specifics). If you want to take the headache out of planning your trip, travel agencies can design and implement your plans for a fee. One tried-and-true group is STA Travel (statravel.com). This organization has been planning adventure travel for over thirty years (I think it made my travel arrangements way back in the day) and has more than 240 branches worldwide.

ACCOMMODATIONS ABROAD

I probably don't need to tell you that these run the gamut from sleeping on somebody's floor to bed-and-breakfasts to four-star hotel rooms; it is just a matter of budget and any lingering pandemic regulations. Hostels are the go-to choice for most students and young people. Not only are they cheap, but they are generally clean, safe, and a way to meet people and make fellow traveling friends. There are youth hostels in almost every major town in every country in every nation around the world. For a directory, go to hihostels.com, the website run by Hostelling International. Airbnb (airbnb.com) lists nightly, weekly, and monthly rentals in more than 180 countries, ranging from shared rooms to entire villas on the seashore. Quality and safety are supposedly guaranteed, but practice caution if you are traveling and staying alone. Homeaway.com and vrbo.com are similar and feature mostly houses and apartments to rent by the week, but if you are traveling with friends and plan on staying in a country for any length of time, they could be a good option.

Another alternative is to stay with a host family in their home or in a dormitory at a local university. Generally these housing options are arranged through a program or travel agency affiliate and are harder to access as a private individual, but you can do it. Cultural Homestay International (chinet.org) and Independent Traveler (independenttraveler.com) are two places to start. You might also be able to arrange a farm stay in rural areas.

WORKING ABROAD

If you plan to stay abroad for a length of time or you want to keep your return open-ended or you just want to get the heck out of here now, you could get a job abroad to pay your way. This is not always easy, and it helps if you already have connections or a job offer from an employer in another country. It's even easier if you have a skill or some previous experience, but this is not necessary. Potential employers include hotels, bars, restaurants, bike repair shops, and computer cafés—you just have to find one with an opening. Do research online, make a list of the possibilities, and write to ask for a job.

It's a good idea to have a clue as to where you will be living, so a potential employer has the secure knowledge that you will show up. Foreign governments also like to know where you are staying ahead of time. An employer who agrees to hire you should send you a letter of employment and the correct paperwork to submit to the government of that country, which will then issue you a visa or permit to work. You will only be allowed a set amount of time to stay in the country and will have to leave when the visa or permit expires. If you get a job through an international work or travel program, your visa or permit will be arranged for you.

Some countries make working as a student really easy—like Australia, which has a great yearlong work visa you can apply for if you are between eighteen and thirty. Other countries make it really hard. And still other countries won't issue a work permit if the government believes its own citizens can fill the job. In this last case, volunteering might be a better option.

WYSE Work Abroad

WYSE Work Abroad is a global nonprofit that places tens of thousands of youth in culturally oriented, quality work abroad and volunteer programs every year. According to the website (wyseworkabroad .wordpress.com), WYSE Work Abroad is the world's leading trade association representing numerous professional organizations in more than 40 countries. To participate in the association, an organization must agree to a code of conduct that protects young workers and volunteers in its employ and promotes foreign work and volunteering as a beneficial form of cultural exchange. The association was formed in 2006 through the merger of the Global Work Experience Association and the International Association for Educational Work Exchange Programmes.

SAFETY ABROAD

As a US teen traveling abroad, you are an easily recognizable target for thieves and criminals. Americans are perceived as being very wealthy. Flashing your designer jeans and expensive logos will make you that much easier to spot. More often than not, criminals will just want to lift your wallet, but some are after your passport, identity and, in the worst cases, you. Be cautious about where you go. Traveling with a friend or a reputable group is the easiest way to protect yourself, but even then things can happen. So be forewarned and prepared. The FBI has a brochure covering the basics of personal safety as a student or young person traveling abroad. You can read it at FBI.gov, but I'll give you the highlights here.

Before You Go

- Leave an itinerary with your family so that they know exactly where you will be staying.
- Familiarize yourself with a country's laws and customs so you can dress and act appropriately. Don't draw attention to yourself or the fact that you are American.
- Assess any major health risks and get appropriate shots and medications. For more information about the precautions to take in different countries, go to CDC.gov.
- Make copies of your passport, driver's license, airplane ticket, and credit cards. Keep one copy at home and carry one copy in your suitcase (apart from the originals).
- Establish points of contact along the way and register your trip with the Department of State at StudentsAbroad.state.gov.
- Pack light in well-organized baggage. Nothing shouts American like being overburdened with stuff. Carrying too many bags makes them easier to steal and makes it harder for you to run, hide, or defend yourself.

When You Get There

- Protect your passport.
- Use only authorized transportation.
- Do not invite strangers into your room, gossip about personal issues, or give out the address of your accommodations in public places.
- Do not carry or flash a lot of cash—be discreet!
- Be courteous and polite, and stay alert, especially on night trains and in sleeping compartments.
- Practice basic safety precautions: lock the doors of hotel rooms

and train compartments, carry valuables and your ID in a front pack or close to your body, and check in often with your parents or other people back home.

WHAT YOU'LL NEED TO GET NOW, BEFORE YOU TRAVEL

This varies depending on where you are going and how long you are away, but the bare bones of travel require the following arrangements in advance of your departure. Use this as a checklist:

- Valid passport and ID
- Travel itinerary with addresses of accommodations, sponsors, and a round-trip flight plan (for visa and customs)
- Visas and permits for various countries
- International driver's license, if applicable
- Shots and prescription medications, if applicable
- Traveler's insurance and traveler's medical insurance (if staying overseas for a while)
- Language prep
- Debit or credit card to withdraw funds in-country
- Contact info for people you can reach out to overseas
- Emergency contact numbers

TRAVEL AT HOME

Can't or don't want to travel overseas? You can still travel domestically. Catch a bus to Montana, learn to ride horseback, see Glacier National Park, and get a job at a local eatery. Save money, and then get a bus ticket home. Or head to another state and do it all over again. Strike out on the Appalachian Trail or Pacific Coast Trail or into one of our national parks and rough it for a month— or a year.

Travel in the contiguous US is as easy as pulling up a map and putting pins in the places you'd like to see. Every state has its own wonders, monuments, and strange mythologies. And you probably don't even have to go that far to do something entirely new. Accommodations can run from your Uncle Joe's spare room to a Motel 6 to a local hostel to a rented room in someone's house. A big plus is that you can walk or bike the expanse of the US, if you have the stamina. Or bus it. Or train it with a USA Rail Pass from Amtrak. Or rideshare and couch surf your way across the country. If you have wheels, you can drive it, listening to a road trip playlist that you will treasure the rest of your life. And you don't have to go alone. Rideshare sites will help you find folks who need a driver or a partner to drive their car across the country, and they pay for gas and lodgings. There's really not that much stopping you—except ICE.

If you are traveling in the US within 100 miles of the border, I have to warn you to bring whatever ID and proof of citizenship you have with you at all times, especially if you are a naturalized citizen. Passport, driver's license, green card, copy of your birth certificate— pack it all and keep copies with your guardians or parents at home. Keep your cell phone charged, and know your rights. ICE officers are prohibited by law from racial profiling, but it's not uncommon. If you get stopped on your travels in the US and you believe you've been the subject of racial profiling, you can file a report with the

ICE office of professional responsibility at ice.gov. My sense is it will go absolutely nowhere, but you never know.

As with everything, practice safety precautions and check references and reviews as part of your planning. On the road, if something or someone feels sketchy, don't stop. Get help. Don't get in anyone's car or allow anyone you don't trust into your car. Here are a few places to start researching a plan:

- Train: amtrak.com
- Bus: greyhound.com, trailways.com, us.megabus.com
- Rideshare: rdvouz.com, shareyourride.net
- Drive someone else's car: myfamilytravels.com/forums (search using the keyword "rideshare")
- Accommodations: couchsurfing.com, airbnb.com, hostels.com

Language Immersion

L anguage immersion is a terrific way to spend your time off, especially since you will gain an extremely marketable skill. Romance languages—French, Italian, and Spanish—are always good to learn, but Chinese, Japanese, German, Arabic, Russian, and languages of emerging markets are going to be in higher and higher demand. And if you can combine a working knowledge of Mandarin or Arabic with some high-tech computer analyst skills, you might have hedge funds (or the CIA) headhunting you.

Any program that sends you abroad, be it for a volunteer, work, or student experience, will also have some kind of language immersion component. But, hands down, the best way to learn a language is to move to the country where it is native and sink or swim.

Aidan Rooney, lead French teacher at Thayer Academy in Massachusetts, has had years of experience taking young people on trips to France so they can cultivate their language skills. He puts it this way:

> The best language immersion programs are the smaller, well-vetted, individuated ones, such that you are in limited contact with your own people and language and peers, and therefore forced to enter the other. It's a bit like traveling, and ultimately best done alone. When we are alone, our vulnerabilities are exposed, and we can fully embrace a foreign culture and language. So, the best program is no program, living with a family or working with regular folk, making new friends and being forced to communicate in the target tongue. The most successful experiences I've orchestrated are one-to-one exchanges between young people: you spend three weeks living with a family in France with someone of similar age, then they do the same *chez toi*. These frequently blossom into family-to-family exchanges, and become, indeed, lifelong relationships. On a personal note, I found myself alone in Paris at sixteen and having to fend for myself, so to speak—make friends, find work, shop, not go too hungry. It was the best language program, one I continued for several years.

Rooney is also in favor of enrolling in a local language class, if you can find one where you will live—especially if you are a newbie to the language. His point, and it is a good one, is that you will learn fast if your survival depends on it. Moreover, you'll learn the local dialect, slang expressions, and shortcuts that a more academic setting can't teach you. Conversation class happens in real time at the bakery, grocery store, or train station.

So the best way to learn a new language is to combine travel, work or study, and full-on immersion with native speakers, living side by side with them. But if you can't do that, there are other ways.

✔ **Don't Miss This: Language Immersion Abroad**

If language study and Europe sound cool to you, check out eurocentres.com. It's a language cooperative that will teach you the language of your choice in almost any European city you want to go to, with homestay options. Or you can look into classes taught abroad by CET (cetacademicprograms.com) in China, Japan, Czechia, Italy, Jordan, Tunisia, and Vietnam. Almost every country where you would want to travel has some kind of academic language immersion program, and you can vet them online before applying. Hebrew in Israel? Try kibbutzprogramcenter.org. Swahili in Zanzibar? Visit world-unite.de. German in a summer? Try the International Summer School of German Language and Culture at ifk.uni-hd.de. Your budget, taste for adventure, and lust for a new language are the only restrictions on what you can do.

You might enroll in a weekly class here at home and enlist your fellow students to meet with you outside of class and speak the language. You can advertise for a native-speaking tutor in your area on Nextdoor.com and then practice at home online or with foreign language software like Duolingo or Rosetta Stone. Or you can join an online language exchange community and find a tutor or study partner in the native country and learn together via video chat, email, text, or phone call.

There are a number of language-focused programs on this hemisphere where you can immerse yourself for a number of weeks. Middlebury Language Schools (Middlebury.edu) at Middlebury College and Mills College (Mills.edu) offer full-immersion programs for high school graduates in ten different languages, including Hebrew, Arabic, Russian, and Chinese. As a current high school student, you can also take advantage of a national program called NSLI for Youth (National Security Language Initiative for Youth; nsliforyouth.org), which gives scholarships and intensive instruction to young people ages fifteen to eighteen to help them learn one of seven high-demand languages, either in the summer or for a full academic year. You could also take a language class at your local community college. It's an easy and affordable way to learn a language and meet like-minded people with whom you can practice.

And don't forget that there might already be a community of native speakers in your own city or town that can help you learn the language of your choice. Where I live (a small New England city), there are over thirty languages spoken throughout my community.

In larger cities, there are going to be even more. You can also listen to streaming radio from your country of interest via the internet. And don't forget your school! There are teachers there who, at the very least, can help you with the Romance languages.

Regardless of how you learn your chosen foreign language, make it a goal to get to a country that speaks it at some time in the near future. Your fluency will grow exponentially while you are there, even if you can only afford to be there for a couple of weeks. Also, know that if you have developed a working knowledge of another language, it will help you get good internships, work, and volunteer positions abroad, so be sure to check out those opportunities too.

✓ Don't Miss This: Language Immersion Online

Here are some online resources to help you with your at-home language immersion. These are open, online experiences with strangers, so practice basic internet safety. Don't send money or give out personal information. Don't engage in or tolerate inappropriate, bullying, or offensive behavior. All these sites are monitored for safety, so report any creeps, misdoings, or scam suspicions immediately.

- En.language.exchange
- Language-exchanges.org
- Mylanguageexchange.com

Mind the Gap

A gap year is distinguished from unscheduled time off in that it is—usually—a set amount of structured time (usually a year) taken by a student between high school and college. Generally, these students have already been accepted to a school and get permission to defer their enrollment for the year to gain real-world experience and take a break from academics. (Because so many students took time off after the COVID-19 shutdowns, some institutions may cap their number of deferments. Always check! Don't assume.) The accepted idea around a gap year is that there is an established date when you will be going back to school. This is not an open-ended arrangement, which makes it much easier for parents to endorse and even fund. As I mentioned in part two, I highly recommend going through the paces junior and senior year and applying to some colleges that you can get into. Once they accept you, you can defer and do your own thing, but this way, you will have your college acceptance to fall back on and your enrollment date to help you structure your time—like a deadline.

Taking time off between high school and college is not only fun but might be the smartest decision you could make for your long-term happiness. Gap years are great antidotes for academic burnout and struggling grades, or if you lack motivation or conviction about getting a college degree. Plenty of graduating teens are taking a gap year now and experiencing real, measurable benefits, including increased self-knowledge, better GPA and graduation rates upon returning to school, and better job satisfaction. People no longer look askance at it, and it is quickly becoming as much the norm as going straight to college. A few dozen detailed guides to planning your gap year have come out in the past few years, including a good one from Lonely Planet called *The Big Trip* that focuses primarily on travel and volunteer opportunities abroad. Companies like the CIEE that used to focus primarily on college students are now expanding their services to include high school students and gap year planning.

There is a formal association that spells out the quantifiable benefits for you and nervous parents. It's the Gap Year Association (americangap.org), and it defines a gap year this way: "A structured period of time when students take a break from formal education to increase self-awareness, learn from different cultures, and experiment with possible careers. Typically these are achieved by a combination of traveling, volunteering, interning, or working. A gap year experience can last from two months up to two years and is taken between high school graduation and the junior year of their higher degree."

The Gap Year Association provides a list of accredited gap year organizations that is growing every month. Holly Bull, president of the Center for Interim Programs, has counseled more than a thousand students through the gap year process. During that time, she has found that the gap year offers creative time to explore areas of interest in a hands-on way and gain clarity regarding what to focus on in college and, ultimately, in the work world after college.

COLLEGE AND REAL-WORLD DISCONNECT

Over the past couple of decades there's been a big push for everyone to go to college right after high school whether they want to or not. It's a dying trend because it doesn't really work or reflect the reality of life after college. According to the National Center for Education Statistics, only 60 percent of incoming freshmen will graduate within six years. And those who do graduate face a job market that is experiencing wage stagnation and, seemingly, has less and less use for a shiny liberal arts degree. According to a 2017 *Forbes* poll, the employment rate of young adults with a BA or graduate degree was 84 percent (though they are not specific about what kinds of jobs graduates are getting). Even so, the cost of living is so expensive due to the burden of student loans and the cost of rent that 56 percent of college graduates are moving back home with their parents, and 24 percent say they plan to stay there until their late 20s or 30s! That's a big disconnect between your investment in your education and outcome, and nobody seems to have real answers for solving it.

Why is college still the default when nearly half of students don't finish, and nearly half of graduates, who have spent a lot of money and time training, can't find work that pays the bills? According to one high school guidance counselor, Doug Drew, the simple truth is that not all of us are meant to be scholars. Nor can most of us afford to be scholars these days. Some of us also need to learn how to be butchers, bakers, candlestick makers, hemp farmers, and river guides. A gap year is a chance to explore other talents and interests unrelated to school (or that can guide your choice of more education) that might have real usefulness, even if only to convince you that what you want is to go back to studying. Drew failed out of college after three semesters and took his own self-designed gap year by cycling alone cross-country for eight months, pedaling directly into the wind. He attributes his ability to go back to college, earn a 3.5 GPA, and graduate with a job to that grinding experience.

Holly Bull puts it this way:

> The gap year provides a sense of relevance . . . to the world. It offers time to rejuvenate after the more onerous aspects of twelve years of schooling. And there is a level of self-confidence and self-knowledge gained through taking on the world outside of the formal classroom that is powerful and unique for one's teens and early twenties. A high percentage of gap year students have a clearer idea of a college major or at least more in-depth knowledge of what they do not want to pursue in college classes. And, on a practical level, students are building a résumé that can help them get jobs down the line.

RISKS OF TAKING A GAP YEAR

What are they? Well, the first one is that you'll spend your time unproductively, and I'm doing my best in this book to ensure that doesn't happen. The second is that you will be out of sync with your peers when you go back to school, but that doesn't seem to be an issue in reality.

Here's Bull on the subject again: "Students are often concerned that they will fall behind their high school classmates or be too old coming into freshman year at college. What they find, however, is that they are really on a parallel track with their college peers and usually encounter other gap year students during their year. If there is a disjoint, it can happen during freshman year because gap year students are invariably more mature and focused compared to their peers."

Another worry is that you will forget everything you learned in elementary school and high school, and flunk out of college. Again, the opposite is more true. Bob Clagett, who worked in Harvard University admissions for years and then served as dean of admission at Middlebury College, found that incoming Middlebury freshmen who took time off between high school and college had GPAs higher than those of their peers right through senior year. He ran the numbers for the University of North Carolina at Chapel Hill, and the GPA results were the same: gap year students surpass their peers throughout their four years of college. Often a gap year will make you choosier and more dissatisfied with college life when you finally go. A year of maturity and growth can make freshmen antics seem pretty stupid,

If you think that a gap year might make sense for you, then it's up to you to decide what the parameters are going to be—where you want to go, what you want to do, and how much you should expect to spend (or need to earn). Beyond that, it's a very open-ended proposition. But in terms of thinking about what you might want to do with this time, there are a few different types of gap year experiences that might help you get your bearings. And don't forget to include both summers.

- Group programs specifically set up for gap year students, where there is often a combination of cultural immersion in another country (or several other countries), language study, service work, and adventure travel. These programs typically run three months to a full year and charge an overarching fee or tuition. Some are academic and more like a study abroad semester. Some of the good ones are Outward Bound (outwardbound.org), National Outdoor Leadership School (NOLS.edu), People to People International (ptpi.org), and Institute for International Cooperation and Development (institute-icd.org/).
- Skill-based options that are often short, intense courses of study, for example, a four-week WEMT (Wilderness Emergency Medical Technician) or TEFL (Teaching English as a Foreign Language) certification course; five weeks of learning how to run a recording studio; four to eight weeks of intensive filmmaking classes; or four weeks of getting a snowboarding teaching certification. Once you have your training, you could then apply

and I know more than a few kids who, after completing a gap year, ended up transferring after freshman year to a school that better suited them. The school they chose in high school just didn't fit who they were anymore.

for an internship that relates to what you've just learned or take your newfound skills on the road. Or start your own creative project based on what you've just learned. Or mix-and-match an intensive with a longer study program somewhere else.

- Internships, apprenticeships, service work, and volunteer options, which are lower cost and more independent than the above programs and are not necessarily with a peer group. They can range from helping kids in a local school in Latin America, to working with primates or penguins in a sanctuary in Africa, to helping out with start-ups, hospitality businesses, journalistic enterprises, event management, and politics.

- Academic programs that can earn you credit for school or give you an alternate education experience. Many museums offer independent study sessions (very much like internships), including the Whitney Museum Independent Study Program in New York City (whitney.org) and the Michigan State University Museum Studies Program (museumstudies. msu.edu), which you can enroll in through their continuing education program even if you aren't a student there. SEA Semester in Woods Hole, Massachusetts (sea.edu), will ship your classes out to sea. If land is more to your liking, you could go on a study program through the School for Field Studies (fieldstudies.org).

The final concern is that you might never go back to school. Researchers Karl Haigler and Rae Nelson studied 280 gap year students from 1997 to 2006 and collected an enormous quantity of data they published in a report called "The Gap Year Advantage" (you can see it at americangap.org). They discovered that nine out

looking back

"I knew I wanted to study abroad; the question was where? Each option seemed more exotic and amazing than the last: Save sea turtles in the Virgin Islands with Student Conservation Association? Yes! Sail around the Caribbean with SEA Semester? Sign me up! Learn to cook in France? Environmental studies in Africa? Anthropology in South America? Data collection in Antarctica? All of the above! When it comes to study abroad options, the world is truly an oyster, and often, the cost is actually less than regular tuition. How would I decide?

"When I didn't get selected for the program in the Virgin Islands, I began to do the requisite soul searching. True, science wasn't really my strong suit. And I get terribly seasick, so SEA Semester probably wasn't a great idea. Did I really want to be a chef? No. What compelled me about Africa aside from loving the books *Heart of Darkness, Out of Africa,* and *West with the Night?* The Mayans always fascinated me, but did I want to be an anthropologist? Antarctica boasted a male-female ratio in my favor, but did I simply want to increase my odds at finding a boyfriend?

"When I really looked at myself, I realized I'd always been interested in philosophy and religion, loved mountains, and for some reason had a fantasy about seeing Mt. Everest. I wanted to live with local families and learn the local language and customs. I also wanted to go somewhere that would inspire me to write. And so I found the School for International Training and the Tibetan Studies program in India, Nepal, and Tibet. And it turned out to be everything I needed to grow in new ways and become who I am, which is the whole point of any study abroad program. Or, as my father said, the best money he ever spent on my education."

—M. Coleman, author

of ten gap year students go back to school within a year. If you wind up being part of the 10 percent who don't, you probably will have found something to do that fulfills you more than studying, which, truth be told, is the essence of getting a life, so you won't care.

PAYING FOR A GAP YEAR

The same rules apply here as they do for traveling. Your gap year can be expensive or cheap, depending on where you go and what you want to do. Working and saving for your gap experience should be part of the overall plan. You might have to work as you go wherever your gap year takes you or you might prefer to get a job and live at home for a set number of months and save up for the rest of the year. At the Gap Year Association website (gapyearassociation .org), you can also find links to scholarships and grants that can help pay for some programs.

When thinking about cost, don't forget to average in what you might save in tuition costs by coming back from your time off re-invigorated and ready to get your degree as efficiently as possible. The less student debt you incur, the better, but if an investment in a gap year leads to a quicker degree, more hands-on experience, and a better job on the other side, the money spent will be well worth it.

Community Development

You don't have to go anywhere to take time off or schedule a gap year experience. Wherever you live, you can find people and organizations in your own backyard in need of your help. In fact, if you're not yet inclined to devote all of your working hours to service as we discussed previously, you can design a hybrid experience by combining a part-time job with community development work as a coach in youth sports, a tutor or mentor to at-risk youth, a volunteer at your local hospital or animal rescue shelter, a community gardener, or a campaigner for a candidate or cause you believe in. You can still take some portion of your time off to travel, but you should not feel like you can't have a fulfilling experience if you want to stay close to home and not expand your carbon footprint.

The goal of community development is to create stability, safety, and economic opportunity where you live. Not only is this a noble goal in and of itself, but it is self-serving in that a more stable community means a better life for you and your family. It is also an inexpensive way to get a lot of hands-on experience quickly and to make good connections with your neighbors. Getting involved with your community can lead to great things. Especially now, when there are so many new grassroots organizations and causes that need your help. Community organizers are the seeds of long-term political and progressive change, and your work in your own community could lead to you making history. Plus, helping and educating the people you have grown up around can feel more satisfying than working with strangers. If you have any political ambitions or a cause you believe in or you simply want to understand the great underpinnings of society, getting involved in the nuts and bolts of community improvement is an important first step.

GRASSROOTS ACTIVISM

Since the 2016 election, there's been a groundswell of popular outrage that has led to the formation of national and local action groups fighting for civil rights, women's rights, prisoner's rights, LGBTQ rights, free and fair elections, the environment, accessible health care, gun regulations, animal welfare, immigrants, small family farms, clean air, safe water, and the public good. Many of these groups are liberal leaning, but there are plenty of bipartisan and more conservative groups on the ground too. The youth activists leading the fight for climate action and gun safety legislation are just the most visible examples of what people your age can accomplish if they have the time and the determination.

No doubt there is a cause you feel strongly about, and likewise, there is probably a group near you holding meetings that you can join right now via Instagram or Facebook. Moreover, there are local, state, and federal issues and campaigns that always need volunteers. In all probability, you or fellow students have participated in some kind of protest action at your school already, so you know what I am talking about. Just pick up your local paper or email your state representative or raise your hand and go to a meeting. The world becomes a different place when everyday people just like you put their energy into changing it.

THE RED CROSS

More than eight hundred Red Cross chapters, located in communities across the United States and its territories, provide a variety of services: blood drives; courses in first aid, CPR, and water safety; connection with family members overseas in the military; assistance in times of disaster; and international tracing and disaster relief. As a young volunteer, you could serve as a member of a local youth council or board or attend a leadership development camp. If you are sixteen or older, you can donate blood or help with blood drives, provide services to veterans and their families, and be trained to lend a hand when disaster strikes. Through the Red Cross, you can get babysitter training and take first aid, CPR, aquatics, and water safety classes. You can also receive training to serve as an instructor or lifeguard.

LITERACY VOLUNTEER

Local and state literacy programs are always looking for new volunteers. In most states, all that is required is a high school diploma or GED and demonstrated proficiency with reading English. The National Literacy Project is an umbrella organization that tracks literacy rates and implements coursework in elementary and secondary schools. You can go to nld.org to search for a program or service in your area and apply to become a volunteer. Alternatively, check out your local library and see how you can help there. Volunteer in the stacks, organize events and readings, read to young children, or help with the annual used book fair. There are many ways your local and school libraries could use your energy. Libraries are a critical and often overlooked gathering place for people of all ages and stages, and they are the treasury of our nation's written history.

FOOD BANKS, MEALS ON WHEELS, HOMELESS SHELTERS, 211 INTERVENTION HOTLINES

It is probably no big surprise that help is needed all over the place when it comes to these charitable services. The best way to find out where they are is to look online. You will need to be trained in 211 crisis intervention services before you begin answering the phone, but anyone over eighteen is welcome.

AT-RISK YOUTH

Become a Big Brother or Big Sister at your local branch of the Boys and Girls Club. Volunteer at the childcare facility of your YMCA or YWCA. Fight violence and drug use in your community by joining DARE (Drug Abuse Resistance Education). Create a SpeakUp! branch in your town to tackle bullying and address issues impacting kids today. Mentor a child at a local arts program or creative writing center. In Portland the Telling Room teaches creative storytelling

looking back

"I became a canvasser with the California League of Conservation Voters because I cared about a few issues that were coming up for referendum in my city. We would meet every day in the afternoons at the headquarters in San Francisco, and then teams of us were shipped out in vans to the suburbs. Our job was to knock on people's doors, give them our spiel, and sign them up to the league. I felt really good about the work I was doing, but knocking on people's doors at dinner time was really hard! They would meet you with an expression like you were carrying the plague. Some just slammed the door. Within days, I figured out which doors to skip, just by the make of their cars and what was on their porch. Sometimes, people were really nice—and it turned out I was really good at getting people to write checks. (We counted our "earnings" in the van on the way back to the city and got paid a commission based on how much we had raised.) It was a lot like being a door-to-door salesperson, only you are selling ideals. I stayed for about three months, through the election, then eventually moved on to work for an advertising company that specialized in political campaigns."

—T. Anderson, media manager

skills to over 2,000 kids a year, and its sister program, 826 Valencia, does the same in many cities across the nation. If you love to act, get involved with a group like the Actors' Gang or the Theatre Lab and help incarcerated youth find their artistic expression through drama.

LOCAL POLITICS

The future of democracy looks like you, and right now you or somebody you know could run for local office. Or maybe there's a red–hot issue in your town you are interested in. Both major political parties, independent parties, the Green Party, and groups concerned with local legislative issues are always on the hunt for volunteers to help them. From creating off-leash dog-walking areas to legalizing cannabis to creating better transportation and housing to running for the school board, you can participate and become a leader shaping the future of your community. Find out who your district representative is and send them an email. Ask them how you can get involved. Young people are in high demand in local politics, so don't feel shy.

COMMUNITY GARDENS

If you live in an urban area, check out the development opportunities at your local community garden or search the directory at communitygardening.org. Growing food for yourself and your neighbors is a fundamental way to connect with people, since we all have to eat. Besides these benefits, learning to grow food will teach you about health, nutrition, farming, delivery systems, and maybe some cooking. You will also be helping to green the landscape and protect the environment. Getting involved doesn't take much skill initially, just a desire to get your hands dirty and your thumb a little greener.

COMFORT KEEPING

These are the services you can perform for specific people in your neighborhood. Maybe an elderly woman needs to be driven to appointments. Or a single mom could use help with shopping or childcare. Or an older couple can't keep up with their lawn or house maintenance. Maybe somebody you know is grieving or alone and would like to spend time with you in a structured way. If

profile

Fred Rogers, TV producer, puppeteer, composer, lyricist, author, children's advocate

Fred McFeely Rogers was born in Latrobe, Pennsylvania, in 1928. After graduating from his local high school, his parents just wanted him to go to college and get a good job. Rogers attended Dartmouth College for one year, and while home on break became fascinated with his parents' brand-new addition: a television set. He transferred to Rollins College in Florida, where he studied music, practiced puppetry, and earned his bachelor's degree in music composition. In 1953 WQED Pittsburgh, the nation's first community-sponsored educational television station, asked Rogers to come work for them, and that's where he first set his sights on creating quality TV programs for the enrichment of children's lives.

One of the first programs Rogers produced was the award-winning show, *The Children's Corner*—a daily, live, hour-long visit with music and puppets. Rogers was the puppeteer, composer, and organist. During that time, he also attended both the Pittsburgh Theological Seminary and the University of Pittsburgh's Graduate School of Child Development. Rogers created *Mister Rogers' Neighborhood* in 1966. It was made available for national distribution two years later, through the organization that would later became the Public Broadcasting Service (PBS).

you can walk or talk, you can probably find somebody who would appreciate your help or attention, and this is a valuable way to spend some of your time off. Ask your parents or a local medical clinic, hospital, or senior center. If you like animals more than people, the local animal shelter always needs volunteers to walk dogs and collect cast-off bedding and linen to use in kennels.

There's a world of want out there that could benefit from your participation. Every moment has the potential to be productive if you just open your mind and put yourself out there. Honestly, you don't know where it will lead and how much it will give back to you—now and down the road.

Conclusion

Here we are, at the end of this book and the beginning of your adventure. When I started revising this edition, I had no idea that a major pandemic would sweep the globe and that much of what I wanted you to learn from these pages—how to be courageous, question authority, take time to know and trust yourself, and invest in your identity and community first—would become lessons the whole world would have to learn. But all of that has happened, and I believe we owe it to all the people who have died to build a better future with what we have learned.

I understand that uncertainty has rained down upon many of you. You don't want it. You never asked for it. And you wish it had never happened. But it has, and here you are. The only question left is, What are you going to do? The universe has conspired with me to encourage you to do your own thing on your own terms. Live boldly and loudly and without fear. I'm not going to tell you that the path ahead will be easy. It never is. You may face financial and technological roadblocks, you may be cheated and afraid and heartbroken, and you will have to work extremely hard. But I know you have the capacity to rise above hardship and find real joy. And purpose. These are the antidote to anxiety and despair, and they are worth taking risks to gain. My best friend tells me over and over again that the proper response to being alive is (in this order): amazement, gratitude, and service—or, "Wow! Thank you! How can I help?"

One of my favorite quotes comes from the film *The Curious Case of Benjamin Button*, written by Eric Roth and directed by David Fincher. The line comes in a voice-over, in a letter from the main character to his daughter: "For what it's worth: It's never too late or, in my case, too early to be whoever you want to be . . . there are no rules to this thing. We can make the best or the worst of it. I hope you make the best of it."

When you look back at these years, I'd like you to be proud of the chances you took. I'd like you to have explored a lot of different experiences and made radical mistakes and met all kinds of people— even ones you really didn't like. I'd like you to be at home in your skin, doing what you love (at least most of the time), surrounded by people and places that inspire you. And I'd like it all to have started here, with the reading of this book. I'd like you to be able to say to yourself: "That's when it all changed for me." And if you do, please write to me and tell me about it.

Wherever you go after graduation, may you blaze a mighty trail.

Resources

This is by no means a comprehensive list of resources (after all, "the future" is a pretty open-ended concept), but it should at least set you on your way. Remember, too, that your school guidance office and your local library are also great places to look around.

Armed Forces

GoArmy.com & GoArmy.com/rotc, Navy.com, Marines.com, AirForce.com, GoCoastGuard.com, USCGA.edu
See what each military branch has to offer.

Civil Service and Community Service

America's Literacy Directory

nld.org
Literacy volunteering in your own state.

Corporation for National and Community Service

NationalService.gov
Includes information about the service program AmeriCorps.

Red Cross

RedCross.org
Disaster relief, CPR training, first aid, blood donation, and emergency preparedness.

Financial Aid, Budgeting, and Scholarships

BalanceTrack.org

Budget and other financial worksheets to keep your money in check.

Cappex.com

Your "headquarters" for college, matching you to the perfect scholarship.

Free Application for Federal Student Aid (FAFSA)

FAFSA.ed.gov

High School Financial Planning Program
HSFPP.org
Topics include planning, borrowing, earning capability, investing, financial services, and insurance.

Scholarships.com/about-us/
Search millions of scholarships and find the college that is your perfect match.

StudentAid.ed.gov/
A comprehensive site explaining all things financial when it comes to college: types of loans, aid, grants and scholarships, and how to qualify for each.

Gap Year
Gap Year Association
All the information, organizations, and listings of programs that you need to convince yourself and your parents that a gap year will be amazing for you.

FieldStudies.org
Study abroad experiences through field-based learning and research.

InterimPrograms.com
A clearinghouse of information about gap years with sample programs and scenarios and the option to schedule a fee-based consultation with an adviser to help you plan.

OutwardBound.org
Experience-based outdoor leadership adventures.

Sea Education Association
SEA.edu
Study at sea for a semester.

The Smithsonian Museum Studies
MuseumStudies.si.edu
Different internships at many of the nation's museums.

Whitney.org

Work closely with professional artists in New York City through the Whitney Museum.

Getting Ready for College

BigFuture.CollegeBoard.org

Start planning, based on grade level, to navigate your life after high school.

CareerOneStop.org

Explore careers and the type of education required for a specific career, along with myriad other possibilities.

CollegeFish.org

Swim around this site to find the right kind of college for you; it's also helpful as a guide to transferring from a two-year to a four-year college.

Independent Educational Consultants Association

IECAOnline.com

IECA can help you determine what you will need in order to be a candidate for college.

StudyPoint.com

Includes SAT, ACT, and other tutoring prep for vital tests you will need for your college submissions.

Jobs and Internships

AFLCIO.org

All about unions and their importance in the American workforce.

GFCLearnFree.org

Teaches computer programs and how to build your résumé.

InternMatch.com

Offers free advice on résumés, cover letters, interview questions, and proper follow-up protocol.

Internships.com

Everything you need to know about internships, including tips and interview prep.

MediaBistro.com

Job listings (including internships), news, education, events, and research for the media industry and media professionals.

Language Immersion

China Educational Tours

CETACAdemicPrograms.com

Semester and summer study abroad programs in Brazil, China, Czechia, Italy, Japan, Jordan, Tunisia, and Vietnam, as well as short-term, customized programs worldwide.

Eurocentres

Eurocentres.com

Learn a language almost anywhere in the world.

International Summer School of German Language and Culture

IFK.uni-hd.de

Study German at Heidelberg University.

Middlebury College

Middlebury.edu

Go deep into a foreign language on the Middlebury campus in Vermont or during the summer on the West Coast at Mills College (mills.edu).

The Mixxer

Language-Exchanges.org

These free educational language exchanges via Skype are hosted by Dickinson College.

My Language Exchange

MyLanguageExchange.com

An online language exchange community.

National Security Language Initiative for Youth
NSLIForYouth.org
Scholarships to study language abroad.

Starting Your Own Business
Entrepreneur
Entrepreneur.com
Online magazine about entrepreneurship.

Score
Score.org
Helps small businesses get started.

The Thiel Fellowship
ThielFellowship.org
This is the place to go to learn more and apply.

US Small Business Association
SBA.gov
Tools to create a business plan, online training, local assistance, and more.

Your Teen Business
YourTeenbusiness.com
A blog designed by a business-minded teen.

Studying Abroad
Association of Foreign Educators
NAFSA.org
Organization of over 10,000 professional members dedicated to serving and advancing the internationalization of higher education. The site has a good explanation of how to get financial aid for foreign study as well.

Center for Study Abroad
CenterforStudyAbroad.com
Pick from a list of countries, each with many programs that are clearly outlined with detailed costs and explanations of courses.

International Studies Abroad
GlobaLinksAbroad.org
This site matches you with a volunteer opportunity in the country of your choice.

Travel
Kayak
Kayak.com
Compare travel sites all at once for flights, hotels, cars, and more.

Student Travel Agency
STATravel.com
Discount student travel agency.

Volunteer, at Home or Abroad
Cross-Cultural Solutions
CrossCulturalSolutions.org
Travel the world, and do good at the same time.

Idealist
Idealist.org
Includes not only volunteer opportunities but job listings and internships.

Visions Service Adventures
VisionsServiceAdventures.com
Participate in meaningful community service in another locale. A very respected nonprofit organization.

VolunteerMatch
VolunteerMatch.org
Find a cause you care about and browse opportunities in your area.

Volunteers for Peace
VFP.org
Become a part of a greater cause by volunteering in another country.

Where There Be Dragons
WhereThereBeDragons.com
Let your dreams be your guide with this long-running favorite program that has taken thousands of teens overseas.

Working Weekends on Organic Farms
WWOOFInternational.org
Live on an organic farm and help native people in a country of your choice.

Work Abroad and Study Abroad
Airbnb
airbnb.com
Unique overnight, weekly, and monthly private home, apartment, and room rentals all over the world.

Center for International Exchange Education
CIEE.org
Work, travel, or study with this internationally renowned student exchange program.

Centers for Disease Control and Prevention
CDC.gov
Diseases and conditions to be aware of while studying abroad.

Couchsurfing
CouchSurfing.com
Find friendly people who will let you stay in their home.

US Students Abroad
StudentsAbroad.state.gov
Travel smart with resources for what to do in an emergency while abroad.

World Youth Student & Educational Work Abroad
WYSEWorkAbroad.org
Opportunities for students to work abroad.

Bibliography

All of these books are tremendously helpful in researching different programs and philosophies around life after high school. I highly recommend all of them.

Baron, Renee. *What Type Am I? Discover Who You Really Are.* New York: Penguin Books, 1998.

Bennet, William J. *Is College Really Worth It? A Former United States Secretary of Education and a Liberal Arts Graduate Expose the Broken Promise of Higher Education.* Nashville: Thomas Nelson, 2013.

Bridges, William. *Transitions: Making Sense of Life's Changes.* Cambridge, MA: Da Capo, 2004.

Gilpin, Robert. *Time Out: Taking a Break from School to Travel, Work, and Study in the US and Abroad.* New York: Simon & Schuster, 1992.

Kepler, Ann. *The Work/Life Balance Planner: Resetting Your Goals.* Chicago: Huron Street, 2013.

Lee, Linda. *Success without College: College May Not Be Right for Your Child, or Right Just Now.* New York: Doubleday, 2000.

Llewellyn, Grace. *The Teenage Liberation Handbook: How to Quit School and Get a Real Life and Education.* Rockport, MA: Element, 1997.

Lore, Nicholas. *Now What? The Young Person's Guide to Choosing the Perfect Career.* New York: Fireside, 2008.

Pink, Daniel H. *A Whole New Mind: Moving from the Information Age to the Conceptual Age.* New York: Riverhead Books, 2005.

Pope, Loren. *Colleges That Change Lives: 40 Schools That Will Change the Way You Think about Colleges.* New York: Penguin Books, 2006.

Selingo, Jeffrey. *College (Un)Bound: The Future of Higher Education and What It Means for Students.* Boston: Houghton Mifflin Harcourt, 2013.

Snyder, Thomas J. *The Community College Career Track: How to Achieve the American Dream without a Mountain of Debt.* Hoboken, NJ: Wiley, 2012.

Unger, Harlow G. *But What If I Don't Want to Go to College? A Guide to Success through Alternative Education.* New York: Checkmark Books, 2006.

Index

About the Author

Photo credit: Charlotte Stone

Genevieve Morgan has made a career out of being an author, editor, and advocate living in Portland, Maine. She graduated with a BA in English from Bowdoin College. After moving to California to pursue an acting career, she wound up instead as a fact-checker at *SF* magazine in San Francisco, quickly rising to become managing editor. She quit that job to work as an editorial assistant in book publishing, eventually becoming the managing editor at Chronicle Books. After a few years, she chucked that job to follow her other dream of becoming a full-time writer and moving to Maine. Today, she lives in Portland with her family and is the author of a beloved children's adventure-fantasy series, *The Five Stones Trilogy* (as G.A. Morgan). She is the editor-at-large for Islandport Books and a frequent contributor to magazine publications where she primarily writes about health, wellness, and—more recently—urban homesteading. Morgan mentors teens and has coached many young adults (and their parents) through the transition from high school to college and beyond. She gave a TED talk based on *Undecided*, which can be viewed on YouTube and welcomes any teen who is struggling with feelings of anxiety, depression, and/or indecisiveness about their future to write her at ga-morgan.com. She is currently figuring out her own next step, which involves another book, growing food, and getting better at playing the guitar.